HOW MONEY WORKS *for the Next Generation*

ACT NOW or pay later

A Stop Being a Sucker® Book

Lauren Mathews **FAIREY** | Christa **MATHEWS**

howmoneyworks.com

We extend our deepest gratitude to Simon Chow, Jane Evans, Matt Luckey, Tom Mathews, Angie McCart, Kim Scouller, Bruce Serbin, and Carlin Wong for their invaluable contributions in making this book possible in every way imaginable. Your dedication, insight, and unwavering support have been instrumental in bringing this vision to life. We are truly grateful for your efforts and commitment to empowering the next generation with financial knowledge.

For more information: licensing@wealthwave.com

Creative direction, design, and production by the WealthWave® Team.

To the Next Generation who is willing to seize
the moment and invest in tomorrow:

This book is for you.

Featuring **TheMoneyBooks** Cast

Zoey - 19, University Student

Zoey can't decide between getting a degree in physical therapy or marine biology. The choice would be simpler if people were as appreciative as animals when you do something nice for them. And by 'people' she means her roommates.

Ashley - 24, Wedding Event Planner

When her entrepreneurial aunt asked her if she had any interest in working for her wedding planning business, Ashley said, "I do." Her aunt—and her clients—rely on her eye for style and telling it like it is. She's not afraid to confront a bridezilla or keep the groomsmen in line. Now if her aunt can just help her find her own Mr. Right...

Maria - 27, CPA, Entrepreneur

Maria believes you can have your cake and eat it too. Which is why she started her own accounting practice for women business owners after being told such a focus wouldn't succeed. Recently engaged, Maria thought the CPA exam was hard, until she started tackling everything involved in planning a wedding.

Hector - 28, Restaurant Owner, Entrepreneur

A born motivator, Hector runs a small fleet of food trucks. Social media made his sandwiches a city-wide success, which is why he named the business, 'Social Sandwich.'

Peter - 30, Food Delivery Driver, Musician

Peter has always been an old soul. He likes old books, old movies, old clothes (he's a thrift store junky), and old music. The only thing you won't get from this trumpet player that's out of date is your takeout order. He supports his budding music lesson business with a food delivery side gig. Just know your corn crab bisque has had an ear full of jazz, soul, and reggae before it ever lands on your table.

Val - 31, Blogger, Social Media Influencer

Four years ago, Val gave birth to a beautiful boy who is on the spectrum. She chose to shift her career from successful interior decorator to the role she was born for—a rising social media influencer who helps others navigate the challenges of raising special needs children.

TJ - 32, Medical Sales

TJ was made for sales and sales were made for TJ. He's got the only infectious things any doctor would ever want in their office—a deadly smile and a killer personality.

Tyler - 35, Industrial Engineer

From engineering solutions, Lego projects with his three kids, and a good dad joke, Tyler knows how to put things together. You'll notice from the pages of this book that he also knows how to put together common sense money concepts. One reason may be that he just started a new business as a financial professional. You go, Tyler!

Leo - 38, High School Principal

Can a principal be liked AND run a tight ship? Ask any of the students at Allmond High School, and the answer is a resounding, "Mr. Leo is the BEST!" Yes, everyone loves Leo—teachers, parents, students, even the guinea pig in Ms. Kinderton's 10th grade Biology class. One of the reasons is that he constantly takes copious notes. Which is also why students agree that, "Mr. Leo never lets you get by with ANYTHING!"

Contents

FIRSTS

Foreword

Writing the foreword for *HowMoneyWorks For The Next Generation: Act Now or Pay Later* fills me with immense pride and a deep sense of purpose. This book, created with love and care by my daughters, Lauren Mathews Fairey and Christa Mathews, is more than a guide to financial literacy—it's a heartfelt message to young people about unlocking their potential and creating a future of confidence and opportunity.

Lauren and Christa grew up immersed in the principles of financial wisdom. Money was never just a topic of conversation at our dinner table; it was a gateway to understanding life, choices, and freedom. From an early age, they witnessed the importance of seeing money not as a source of stress, but as a tool for empowerment—a way to build dreams, help others, and craft the life they envisioned.

Their journey with money, nurtured over years of learning and application, shaped them into the remarkable people they are today: women who not only understand how money works, but who live with the confidence and clarity that comes with financial literacy. They are living proof that teaching these principles early can change the trajectory of a life.

This book is their gift to the next generation. It's written with a voice that speaks directly to young minds, making the concepts of money approachable, relatable, and even fun. It's not just a guide—it's an invitation to see financial knowledge as an essential part of self-discovery and independence. Lauren and Christa's goal is simple yet profound: to spark a curiosity in young people about money and to equip them with the tools to make smart choices now that will pay dividends for a lifetime.

As James Clear, author of *Atomic Habits*, says:

"You do not rise to the level of your goals. You fall to the level of your systems."

This book is your system. It's your roadmap to understanding how money works, so you can rise to your highest potential.

Parents, educators, mentors—we hold the key to shaping the future by equipping young people with the tools to thrive. I encourage you to join us in this mission. Share this book, discuss its lessons, and help the young minds in your life discover the power of financial literacy.

To the young readers holding this book: this is your starting point. Dive in, embrace the journey, and take charge of your future. The power to shape your life is in your hands—and it starts here.

Here's to building a generation that not only knows how money works but knows how to make it work for them.

Tom Mathews

TOM MATHEWS

Lauren and Christa's father, Author of HowMoneyWorks: Stop Being a Sucker; Change Your Literacy, Change Your Life: Begin Your Personal Financial Revolution; *and* Aim for the Heart

Introduction

> “
> **The more you learn, the more you earn.**
>
> – WARREN BUFFETT

The title of this book is *How Money Works for the Next Generation: Act Now or Pay Later.* Within this title lies the essence of what we will cover. You'll learn how money really works, and why starting to build your financial future as soon as possible is crucial—otherwise, you risk missing out. These are the central themes of the book, but what about the term 'Next Generation?' The next generation is anyone just beginning to take personal responsibility for their financial well-being.

Maybe you're 18, navigating the rising costs of education and thinking about what career path to pursue.

Maybe you're 27, having just completed your doctorate—a tremendous accomplishment—yet you're left wondering why years of schooling didn't teach you how to manage student loans or make smart insurance decisions.

Maybe you're 32, married for two years, and now expecting your first child. You and your spouse are ready and motivated to buckle down and get serious about your financial planning.

Whoever you are, whatever your age, if you're at a stage where you're starting to take control of your financial future and need some direction, you're holding the right book. We're here to help you navigate the basics, using clear, straightforward language you won't have to Google later. It doesn't need to be complicated. In fact, we've been careful to explain these concepts in a way that's both simple and thorough.

You don't need a Ph.D. in finance to understand this book. You just need the desire to make informed, confident choices. Who doesn't want to be a smarter decision-maker when it comes to money?

It's never too early—or too late—to start mastering your finances.

Don't worry about feeling behind or stressed over what you should have done years ago. If you're stepping into adulthood and reading this book, you're exactly where you need to be. Being young gives you one of the greatest advantages in the world: **time.** You'll see just how big of a deal that is...

We believe there are two key steps to achieving financial peace: education and action. Fortunately, this book covers the education part of that equation.

Money can seem overwhelming, but we want you to hear this loud and clear: we believe in you. All it takes is an opportunity to be introduced to this information, and then you can begin making it work for your life.

So, here we go! Turn the page, start reading, and get excited—your financial future is about to look very different.

You've got this!

– Lauren & Christa

REALITIES

Financial Literacy is a Human Right

Financial Illiteracy is the #1 Economic Crisis in the World[1]

"

Financial illiteracy is not an issue unique to any one population. It affects everyone: men and women, young and old, across all racial and socioeconomic lines. No longer can we stand by and ignore this problem. The economic future of the United States depends on it.[2]

– PRESIDENT'S ADVISORY COUNCIL ON FINANCIAL LITERACY

Financial illiteracy traps more than half of American adults[3] in cycles of poverty and survival. Without the tools to manage, protect, and grow money, economic inequality deepens, progress stalls, and communities continue to suffer. **Financial literacy is a foundational human right, essential for empowering you to take control of your future and help your family and community thrive.** By prioritizing it, you can be part of the solution to break these cycles in your own life and create a more prosperous world for everyone.

Imagine if understanding how money works was as essential to your education as reading, writing, or math. What if concepts like the Rule of 72, Compound Interest, and the Time Value of Money were things everyone learned before they became adults—just like learning how to do your laundry or drive a car? This isn't some far-off dream; it's something that should be a basic human right. Financial literacy isn't just for the rich or those with fancy degrees—it's something everyone needs to navigate the world we live in.

The truth is, not understanding how money works can limit your options in ways you might not even realize. You might be making financial decisions right now that are holding you back without even knowing it. It's not just about knowing how to budget or invest—it's about being confident in your choices, knowing you're not just guessing your way through life. When you learn the basics of personal finance, you're gaining more than knowledge—you're gaining the power to make decisions that will impact your future and help you reach your goals.

Think about it: we teach kids how to read and write because it's essential to participating in society. Well, financial literacy should be just as fundamental. Without it, you're starting behind. Not knowing how to manage debt, save, or make appropriate investment choices can seriously limit your opportunities—and impact everything from your mental health to your overall sense of security. Financial decisions are a huge part of life, and the sooner you learn about them, the better you'll be at setting yourself up for long-term success.

This is why financial literacy isn't just a 'nice-to-have' skill—it's a life skill. Learning how to budget, save, and invest shouldn't be reserved for the wealthy or those in high-paying jobs. These concepts should be available to everyone because they're the foundation of financial freedom and security. When you understand how to make your money work for you, instead of working for your

Imagine navigating a foreign country without your maps app. An exciting adventure can quickly become a hazardous ordeal. That's how essential financial literacy is to a person's life. When you have no GPS for the financial road ahead, you can quickly become... very lost.

money forever, you change the whole trajectory of your life. Imagine being able to make decisions that help set you up for financial success, instead of constantly worrying about debt or missed opportunities. Plus, constant worrying... well, we all know that can lead to health issues.

Just like income, education, and employment, financial capability is a separate and important socioeconomic indicator of health.[4]

At the heart of financial literacy is empowerment. It gives you the knowledge to break free from financial stress, avoid debt traps, and make decisions that will set you up for the future you want. For example, when you understand the power of compound interest (which we'll cover in the Concepts section), you can use it to grow your savings and investments, setting yourself up for long-term wealth—and health.

Learning about money also helps level the playing field. When everyone has access to financial education, we create a society where success isn't determined by your bank balance or family background. Financial education gives you the tools to manage your money, build wealth, and create a more secure future—things that should be available to everyone. Without financial education, the gap between the financially savvy and the financially ignorant only grows, leaving too many people stuck in a cycle of financial struggle.

You already know that financial decisions are everywhere—from paying off student loans to deciding whether to rent or buy a home to thinking about retirement. Financial literacy isn't optional—it is essential for navigating the world we live in. When you view financial literacy as a fundamental human right, you're not just taking control of your own future—you're becoming part of a movement that empowers everyone to make informed financial choices, build wealth, and create long-term security.

This book is your gateway to that transformation. As you dive into the pages, you're not just learning about personal finance—you're claiming your right to a more secure, confident financial future. The time to take control of your money is now, and with the tools you'll gain here, you'll be ready to make empowered, confident decisions every step of the way.

ACT NOW

- ✓ Recognize that financial literacy is a core life skill.
- ✓ Think of it as incredibly empowering.
- ✓ Embrace it for the sake of your wealth... and health.

PAY LATER

- ✗ Put off learning financial literacy concepts and run the risk of finding yourself financially lost.
- ✗ Remain in denial that you have power over your financial future.

REALITIES

‘How Money Works’ Is Not Taught In Schools

With the awareness that financial literacy is a foundational human right, your next question might be, "If it's such a core life skill, why isn't it taught in schools?"

Great question. The reason is a bit counterintuitive but makes total sense when explained. To get there, however, we'll need to reverse-engineer this puppy.

Tyler, you nailed it. And, TJ, you know what we meant.

An argument can be made that it's more about corporate profit and political agendas. Is it really so shocking that the ones behind financial literacy not being taught in schools may be the big institutions prioritizing their agendas over consumers?

Think about it... Why would the rich and powerful lobby for financial education in schools when that would create tens of millions of financially empowered consumers making smarter financial decisions?

Under this theory, when people make wiser spending choices, big brands earn less from expensive lattes, lavish clothes, fancy cars, and luxury apartments. Banks profit less from all the dumb-dumbs (hey, they actually give you a sucker) who stash their money in low-interest-yielding savings accounts. Credit card companies collect fewer fees, and governments receive less tax revenue.

Our goal is to help more people build better lives for themselves instead of building bigger towers for industries. When corporations and policymakers aren't the only ones who understand how money works—when personal finance becomes a central part of high school education and universities—the playing field levels. They may get less, but you get to keep more.

> **College graduates spent 16 years gaining skills that will help them command a higher salary, yet little or no time is spent helping them save, invest and grow their money.**
>
> - VINCE SHORB, CEO, NATIONAL FINANCIAL EDUCATORS COUNCIL

Now you know the ugly reason why you didn't learn about money in school. It's an even harder pill to swallow when you consider all the knowledge you were taught but never use. Take the Pythagorean theorem. When was the last time you had to measure the hypotenuse of a right triangle? There are countless other examples of skills you were required to learn but will never use in real life.

Currently, only 26 states require a personal finance class for high school graduation.[5] While progress has been made, there's still a long way to go. For many of these required finance classes, the material can be outdated, obsolete, or incomplete—with the curriculum often being far too basic to help adults effectively manage their earnings, savings, and investments.

Every student—especially those entering adulthood—needs to know the basics: budgeting, investing, debt management, and compound interest. Beyond these core concepts, every high schooler should have a working knowledge of the critical action steps to take for each stage of life, from college to career to retirement. The impact of this would be transformative to our society.

For those of us who weren't taught about money in school, how do you catch up? You must commit yourself to increasing your financial literacy (this book is a great start) and find a financial professional to guide you (we'll talk more about that later). But first let's have a conversation with our high school principal, Leo...

A Conversation

WITH LEO—OUR HIGH SCHOOL PRINCIPAL

Leo, you're a cast member of the book and a really good friend. Thanks for taking a few related questions from your perspective as a high school principal!

It's my pleasure, Maria. Just remember I don't make policy. I just try to make sure things run smoothly.

Which is no small job. Let's start with the big one. Why don't all 50 states teach personal finance in high school and—for those that do—why isn't the curriculum more complete?

In 2020, only 8 states required a personal finance class for graduation.[6] Today, more than half of all states have this requirement. It's happening but policies take time to put in place.

Well, THERE'S a political answer. Isn't it because the industry and the government team up to keep people financially illiterate?

OK, now! Val comes out swing'n. It certainly is suspect that such a critical life skill gets so little support from all the departments of education. But to be fair, we have very little interest from students in the single class we do offer. Maybe that's part of it...

I know it's not your fault, Leo, but it just doesn't add up. It's almost as bad as not teaching our kids to read or do basic math. And, blaming it on the interest of the students—seriously? Maybe, nationwide, the classes are just... lame.

I remember I took a personal finance class in high school and it was basically about how to open a checking account, balance a check book—and the dangers of credit cards. Had earbuds in the whole time! S'where I got reeaalllly deep into Bebop Jazz.
Hold up, Peter—we talk'n Gillespie or Coltrane? 'Cause either way—I got you! Sounds like personal finance wasn't a favorite class...
That's cool, Leo. Charlie Parker was more my jam. And the class? Hated it. It was soooo boring—it all felt theoretical 'cause I was like 16 and had like zero money.
Would you have enjoyed it more if you learned how to build and protect wealth—manage debt, create cash flow, and establish an emergency fund?
Wait, how to 'build wealth?' Dude—sign me up! I wanted to be smart about money—and rich—haha. I was just a broke kid. The class could've been so much cooler and more engaging.
I hear you, Peter, but I just don't have that kind of class to offer.
Leo, what if the class was a seminar or course offered to students, parents, and teachers by community partners?
Interesting, Maria—as in local professionals? Well see now, I could do that all day long!
Exactly, that's a way of solving the problem without fixing the system. That's our time! This was productive, Leo. Thank you.
You're all very welcome.

ACT NOW

- ✅ Resolve yourself to gain the education you weren't given.
- ✅ Take full responsibility for your financial education.
- ✅ Allocate time not just to read this book, but to study it.

PAY LATER

- ❎ Allow personal finance to intimidate you.
- ❎ See yourself as a victim of an insufficient education.
- ❎ Believe that you're unable to take control and master your money.

REALITIES

If You Don't ACT NOW, You Will PAY LATER

The Next Generation's Greatest Financial Advantage

Time is everything—regarding personal finance. You've probably heard phrases like "Time is money," "Time flies," and "Time is slipping into the future." They're all true—and they should serve as both a motivation and a warning for young adults, from late teens to people in their later 30's.

When you're young, your greatest asset is time. It's your most valuable treasure, your superpower, and the crown jewel of your financial future. Time is the one thing older generations would do anything to get back. It's a precious resource that, once lost, can't be regained.

Picture it: Time, radiant and full of potential, sits on a pedestal in the vault of your youth, waiting for you to unlock its power. When you pair it with the money you earn—even small amounts—it becomes the heart of your entire financial strategy, capable of producing security, opportunity, and independence for every stage of life. No other financial vehicle has that kind of potential.

But there's a catch—and it's a big one.

Every day you wait, that brilliant asset of time gets a little bit smaller. It fades, and one day, when you finally realize its true value, you'll look back and see that it no longer has the massive potential it once did. What was once the Hope Diamond of your financial portfolio now requires a magnifying glass to inspect. You'll regret the moments you let slip by. You'll wish you could turn back time when it gleamed bright with possibilities, urging you not to ignore it—pleading with you to ACT NOW.

Waiting to get started is one of the most expensive things you can do. Being young means you have one of the greatest assets in the world on your side: TIME.

Maximize a Powerful Force of Wealth-Building

Time empowers you to maximize one of the most powerful forces in wealth-building—compound interest. By starting early, even small, consistent investments can grow exponentially over decades. This advantage can transform modest contributions into significant wealth, providing financial independence and security in the future.

Time works as a multiplier. The earlier you start saving and investing, the longer your money has to grow. For example, if a 25-year-old invests $200 a month with a 7% annual return, they could amass over $500,000 by the time they're 67. In contrast, someone who starts at age 35 would need to invest nearly double to achieve the same result. This demonstrates how time, combined with consistent action, can yield life-changing outcomes.

To make the most of these potential outcomes, you must take action right away. Waiting not only wastes the potential of compounding but also increases the financial burden later in life. Let the thought of scaling back your future lifestyle, watching others enjoy freedoms you can't afford, and working into your retirement years, motivate you to take action.

As if maximizing the power of compounding weren't enough, when you take action now, at a young age, you have the chance to enjoy all the benefits of living with your financial house in order. By focusing on the right short-term financial goals—like managing debt, building an emergency fund, increasing your cash flow, and establishing healthy spending and budgeting habits—you'll position yourself to enjoy life's big moments, like buying a car or a house, raising children, taking vacations, and giving back to your community.

Acting now allows you to maintain control and discipline over your finances, which can lead to less anxiety and greater peace of mind. By taking proactive steps, you'll prevent financial challenges from piling up, enabling you to enjoy lasting financial well-being at every stage of life.

There are no sane reasons to wait, Val, but let's look at the obstacles that hold many people back.

Common Barriers to Acting Now

Many young adults encounter obstacles that keep them from taking the first step toward financial success. Identifying which barriers are holding you back is the first crucial step. Once you understand what's causing your inaction, partnering with a financial professional can provide the guidance and support you need to overcome those challenges and move forward with confidence.

Which of these barriers are holding you back?

Information Overwhelm

The vast amount of financial advice available (especially online and on social media) can feel confusing and paralyzing.

Procrastination

Delaying saving and investing is common, with many thinking they'll have time later—time that slips away quickly.

Lack of Financial Education

Without a foundational financial education, the importance of starting early may not be apparent or seem important.

Waiting for Guidance

Many hesitate to act, rather than proactively seeking help from a financial professional.

Fear of Mistakes

Concerns about making poor financial decisions, with hefty consequences for 'screwing up,' often lead to inaction.

> **"Look, if you had one shot, or one opportunity. To seize everything you ever wanted in one moment. Would you capture it or just let it slip?**
>
> – EMINEM

The cost of inaction is steep. Delaying investments means having to save much more later to achieve the same financial goals. Young adults who put off saving may struggle to afford the lifestyle they envision or delay retirement altogether. They risk living paycheck to paycheck, burdened by financial stress, while watching peers who took action enjoy more independence and security.

The good news is that overcoming these barriers is entirely possible. With a little effort to increase financial literacy, young people can develop confidence and clarity about how to start preparing for the future. Seeking guidance from a financial professional can simplify the process, ensuring their plans align with long-term goals. Small, consistent contributions to investment accounts, such as retirement plans or brokerage accounts, are the building blocks of future wealth.

Acting now doesn't require vast resources—just the willingness to start. By committing to financial growth today, young adults can help build towards a more secure life they desire and avoid the regret of squandered time. The message is clear: take advantage of your greatest asset—time—and let it work for you. The sooner you start, the more you'll gain, and the brighter your financial future will be.

ACT NOW

- ✓ Identify and remove any barriers that hold you back.
- ✓ Find a financial professional to help guide you.
- ✓ Set a date on your calendar to take action as soon as possible.

PAY LATER

- ✗ Ignore the real opportunity that passes with every day you wait to get started.
- ✗ Allow procrastination and overwhelm to block you from all the potential you possess today.
- ✗ Miss out on the amazing things the power of compound interest can do for your financial future.

CONCEPTS

The Power of Compound Interest

At this point, we hope you're fired up! But before we discuss action steps, it's crucial to understand a few core concepts that will guide all the major money moves you make. Without this foundational knowledge, you risk misfiring and making mistakes that could have long-lasting consequences.

Armed with these principles, however, you'll gain the confidence to help hit your targets and achieve your financial goals. These concepts will provide you with invaluable insights to cut through marketplace biases, internet noise, and social media misinformation, allowing you to navigate your financial journey more successfully.

Think of learning these concepts like planning a wedding. Before the big day, countless details must be considered: an unforgettable venue, the perfect cake, the right photographer, the rehearsal dinner, the ceremony itself, and the reception. Without proper planning, the event could easily turn into a disaster or a huge disappointment. You need to understand how to plan everything—and then follow through with the work. Only then can you hope for a successful and joyful event.

It's the same with your financial plans—except the event is your life. You need to get it right so your life unfolds in the way you're dreaming it will. The concepts you're about to learn will serve as the foundation for your financial strategies and help you plan your financial future with purpose and clarity.

In the next four chapters, you'll discover the fundamentals of how money works. Then, you'll 'marry' these concepts to the essential financial skills you'll use throughout your life.

Let's start with the first concept:

What is interest? Interest is the cost of borrowing money. Simple, right?

What most people don't realize, however, is that interest can work for you or against you.

The compound interest illustrations provided in this chapter are for informational purposes only and are based on hypothetical assumptions. Actual results may vary due to factors such as interest rate fluctuations, fees, taxes, and market conditions. These illustrations do not constitute financial, investment, or legal advice, nor do they guarantee future performance.

Fair question, Zoey. Let's make it clear by breaking it down a little bit...

When you deposit your money with a financial institution, you earn interest. When you borrow money from them, they earn interest.

When you deposit money into a savings or checking account with a bank or financial firm, the bank may use your money to make loans to other customers in order to make investments and generate profits for themselves and their shareholders. In return for using your money, they pay you interest. **This is an example of interest working for you.**

On the other hand, when you borrow money—like taking out an auto loan or a mortgage for a house—you're using the bank's funds to make your purchase (assuming you don't pay up front with cash). In this case, your monthly payments include interest, which is the cost of borrowing their money. **Here, interest works against you.**

Simple Interest Compared With Compound Interest

Pip, from the Dicken's novel *Great Expectations*, received interest-free money from his benefactor, Miss Haversham (he *was* required to marry her ward, Estella, which complicated things... a lot). Harry Potter was left oodles of wealth from his deceased parents. Even in the real world, well-off parents often fund their kids' college education and gift them assets like cars.

If you don't have a benefactor like Pip or Harry, you will likely need to borrow money along the way. This means you'll be paying interest.

There are two types of interest—simple interest and compound interest.

Simple interest is a method of calculating interest where the amount earned or owed is based only on the original principal amount, not on accumulated interest. This type of interest remains constant over time.

Simple Interest = Your Principal × Interest Rate × Time

Simple interest is typically used with auto loans and personal loans. To see how simple interest works, let's take a look at an elementary example of a personal loan from a family member.

Let's say you borrow $1,000 from your Uncle Jack and he charges you 2% simple interest annually until you can pay him back. 5 years later, you have some cash, so you return the principal plus simple interest. Since 2% of $1,000 is $20, you'd pay him a consistent rate of $20 per year. The total you'd pay Uncle Jack is $1,000 + ($20 x 5) =$1,100. Let's see what it looks like on a chart:

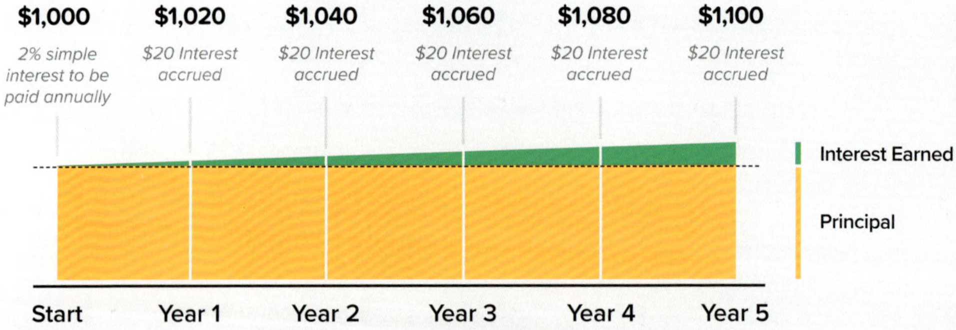

Compound interest, on the other hand, is the interest calculated on both the initial principal and the accumulated interest from previous periods. It allows your money to grow faster over time, as the interest earns interest.

When you see the growth curve possibilities of the power of compound interest compared with simple interest, it almost seems too good to be true.

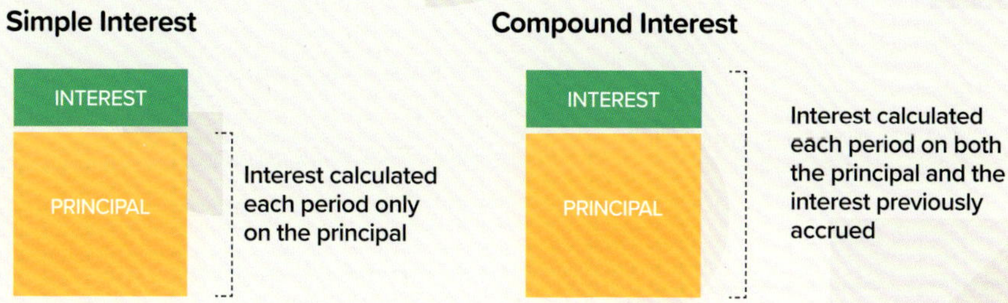

Let's visualize how the exponential growth potential of compound interest—where interest is earned on both the principal and accrued interest—outshines the linear growth of simple interest, which only accrues based on the principal.

An account is opened with $500 and each month $500 is added to the account. For 45 years, the money compounds monthly at a 9% constant annual interest rate.[7]

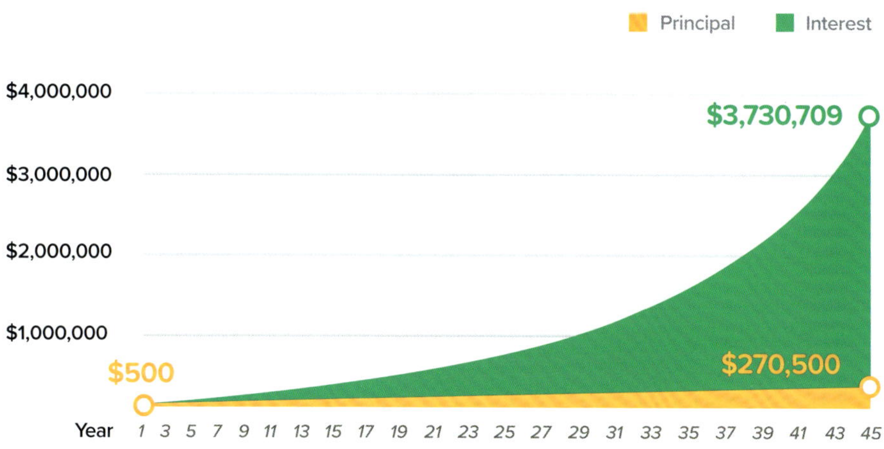

Notice, it's the interest earned that creates significant growth, not the $270,000 of savings added. This is the power of compound interest.

> **"**
>
> **Compound interest is the eighth wonder of the world. He who understands it, earns it; he who doesn't, pays it.**
>
> – ALBERT EINSTEIN

Saving money every month always makes a difference.

Let's say that one day Tyler opens a savings account with $50,000 but never adds another dime to the account. On the same day, Maria opens the exact same type of account with $500 and then adds an additional $500 every month. Both accounts earn a constant 9% annual interest rate.[7]

After 45 years, whose account is worth more—Tyler's or Maria's?

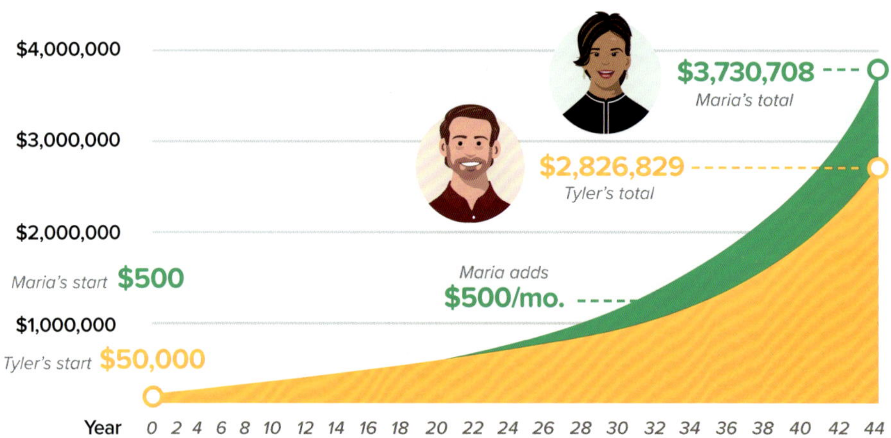

With only $500 at the start, Maria earns more! Regardless of how much you have to start with, consistent savings each month can make a big difference.

Compounding and time both matter. But what about the rate of return—does that matter? Oh, yeah!

Take a look at the growth curves below. They each reflect $178 added each month to an annual compounding account beginning at age 25 and then growing until retirement—age 67.[7] The chart shows the interest rate growth for 1%, 3%, 6%, and 9%. Observe how significant the spike in growth can be when your rate of return is just a few percentage points higher. Compounding, time, and your interest rate all influence how hard your money can work for you.

Once you see the difference, it's hard to imagine intentionally placing money earmarked for longer term goals at 3% or 1% or less, yet it happens every day.

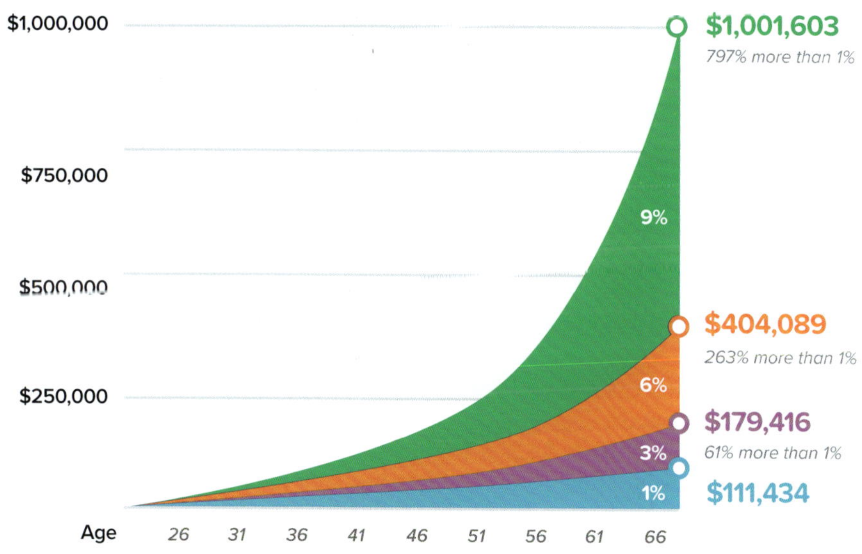

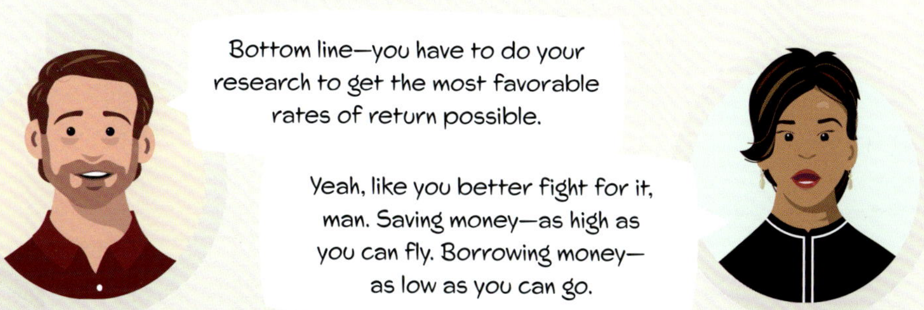

Considerations for when interest is working AGAINST you...

Credit Card Debt (COMPOUND INTEREST)

Credit card interest adds up fast if you don't pay off your balance each month. If you're late on payments, your rate will skyrocket, making everything way more expensive.

Try calling your credit card company and ask if they can lower your rate—it works more often than you think.

Student Loans (TYPICALLY SIMPLE INTEREST, BUT CAN BE COMPOUND)

Federal loans have set interest rates, but private ones can change and get more expensive over time. Refinancing might save you money, but be careful—you could lose perks like payment breaks.

Watch for forgiveness programs or better rates to refinance when the timing's right.

Payday Loans (SIMPLE INTEREST)

Payday loans charge insanely high fees, so you end up paying back way more than you borrow. If you roll it over or delay paying, the costs pile up super quickly and trap you in a cycle.

Avoid these if at all possible. If not, look for cheaper options, like borrowing from a credit union or a trusted family member.

Auto Loans (SIMPLE INTEREST)

A high-interest car loan could mean you'll be paying way more than the car is worth. Dealerships might push their financing, but it's not always the cheapest choice—check out local banks and credit unions.

Pay off your auto loan faster to reduce the total interest you'll pay over the life of the loan.

Home Mortgages (SIMPLE INTEREST)

Even a small difference in the mortgage rate can make your house cost way more in the long run. Loans with adjustable rates might start cheap but can get more expensive later.

Save up for a bigger down payment—it can help you lock in a lower interest rate.

Considerations for when interest is working FOR you...

Financial Professionals

Working with a financial professional is crucial when evaluating interest rates for growing your money. They can help you explore a full range of products and services you may not be aware of.

Be transparent with your financial professional about your goals and current situation to get customized options. To start the process of finding a financial professional, ask the person who gave you this book—or get a recommendation from a parent, family member, or trusted friend.

Fixed vs. Variable

When choosing a savings or investment account, consider whether your principal can fluctuate, as this impacts long-term growth. Assess your goals and financial situation, and consult a financial professional to find the option that satisfies your needs.

There are a lot of factors to consider, like how long you have to invest and how much risk you are comfortable with.

Shop Around

To secure competitive interest rates for your savings and investment vehicles, compare offers from various financial institutions. Remember, you're not obligated to stay with your current bank.

Don't be afraid to negotiate terms with financial institutions by asking for better interest rates or lower fees.

Projections

Before opening a savings or investment account, run projections on the expected rate of return over the duration your money will remain in the account, considering factors like fees and potential rate changes.

Ask your financial professional for help in reviewing historical performance and evaluating future projections.

Easy Access

How easily you can access your money is called liquidity. If quick access is a priority, you may need to settle for a lower interest rate, as higher yields often come with restrictions.

Be mindful of the penalties you could face for withdrawing your money early from less liquid accounts.

ACT NOW

- ✓ Find a financial professional to guide you with your financial decisions.
- ✓ Identify all the ways money is working for or against you right now.
- ✓ Work with your financial professional to move your money to saving vehicles or loans with more favorable interest rates and terms.

PAY LATER

- ✗ Think to yourself, "interest rates sound complicated and boring—it's probably not that big of a deal."
- ✗ Put your money into a low interest savings account without considering other options that can offer higher returns and better terms.
- ✗ Base your decision to get a car loan or mortgage solely on your monthly payment, not on the interest rate.

CONCEPTS

The Time Value of Money

The Time Value of Money is a fundamental concept that emphasizes the greater worth of money available today compared to the same amount in the future.

This idea stems from the fact that money you have now can be invested to grow through interest or other returns, increasing its value over time.

To visualize this, let's imagine a simple scenario with Tyler.

Tyler has a $100,000 lump sum earning compound interest. He plans to save the money until he reaches the retirement age of 67. What is the time value of his money if he starts saving it at the age of 35? What would it be if he starts at 45... or 55? The VALUE of the money remains the same at all three ages—$100,000. But the TIME VALUE depends on how many years it has to grow. Take a look...

Tyler at 35

TIME VALUE =

$100,000

\+ **32 years to save**

Tyler at 45

TIME VALUE =

$100,000

\+ **22 years to save**

Tyler at 55

TIME VALUE =

$100,000

\+ **12 years to save**

The most time value your money will ever have is right now. With every day you wait, the time value of your money slips away like sand through an hourglass. **This is why it is so important to ACT NOW.**

1 Difference—3 Very Different Outcomes

We've been repeating the theme of this book—that time is one of the greatest resources you have as an investor. Proper investing is a long-term game, played over your entire life. Consider the chart below to see how important the element of time is in your financial future...

How this chart works: [8]

- Three people invest $1,000 initially.
- They each add $100 per month until they turn age 67, each earning 7% per year.
- The only difference is that one person starts investing at age 32, another at 27, and the third at 22.

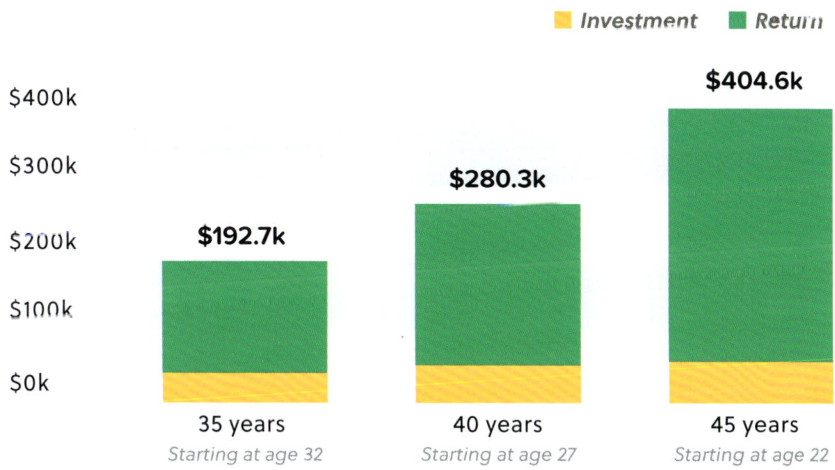

Consistently investing $100/month could increase to $400,000 within 45 years. You would cut that amount by more than half if you shorten that window by just 10 years.

The Longer You Wait, The More You Must Save

The time value of money delivers one urgent message: start saving early—no matter how young you are. If you're 18 or 20, setting aside just $100 a month (even if you need a side gig to make it happen) and letting compounding do its thing, that $100 could turn into a small fortune by retirement. However, every year you delay means having to save more to reach the same goal.

Wait too long, and the time value of money can dwindle to zero. Many people approach retirement with no savings, realizing too late that there's no time left to harness the power of compounding or build the income they need.

Will you answer the time value of money's call to start saving now and unlock compounding's potential? For those in their teens to late 30s, the good news is that time is still on your side. For those 40 to 60, the message is more urgent. The chart below highlights the opportunity—ACT NOW to let the time value of money work for you.

How much do you need to save monthly to have **$1,000,000** by retirement?[7]

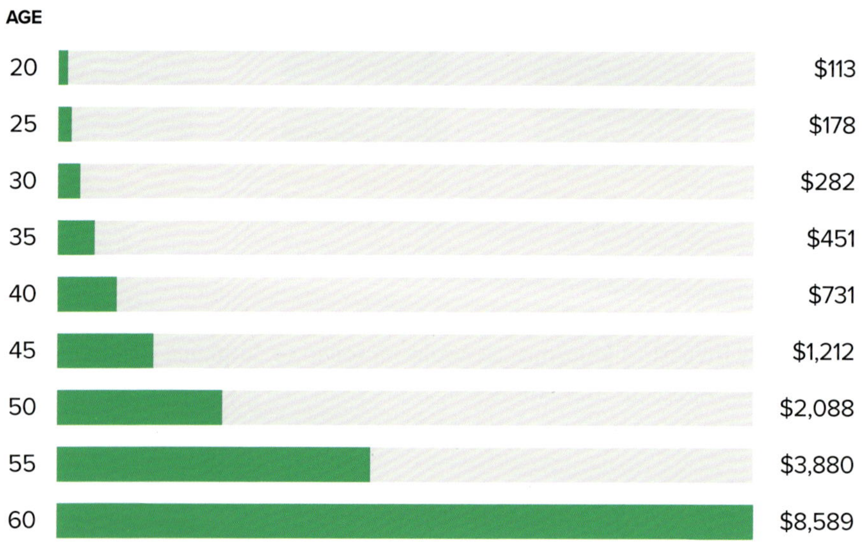

Assumes a 9% average annual interest rate, compounded monthly, and a retirement

Make The Commitment to Yourself to ACT NOW

Fill in the blanks below to start saving at your current age, without letting another year—or another day—slip by.

What's your current age?

Based on the chart on the previous page, how much do you need to start saving each month to have about $1,000,000 by retirement?

What's the monthly amount if you wait 5 years?

Pay it forward! Name a few friends or family members you think can benefit from this idea.

Check the following. To leverage the time value of money, I will...

Start Now

Now is always the best time to start.

Save Regularly

Get the highest interest rate possible.

Be Patient

Good things come to those who wait.

ACT NOW

- ✓ Start saving and investing today—even small amounts add up over time.
- ✓ Understand that every dollar you delay investing is a missed opportunity for future growth.
- ✓ Work with a financial professional to identify high-impact strategies that maximize the value of your money over time.

PAY LATER

- ✗ Assume there's plenty of time to start saving and miss out on years of compounding growth.
- ✗ Spend without a plan, ignoring how today's choices reduce your future financial potential.
- ✗ Procrastinate, thinking you'll 'catch up later,' and make achieving financial goals significantly harder.

CONCEPTS

The Rule of 72

DISCOVER

THE Rule OF 72

Though it may seem like magic, the Rule of 72 is a simple mental math shortcut that can be used to approximate the number of years it will take for your money to double.

How simple is it? Voila!...

72 ÷ Interest Rate = Years to Double

The Rule of 72 is a mathematical concept that approximates the number of years it will take to double the principal at a constant rate of return compounded over time. The interest rates referenced are for illustrative purposes only and do not represent actual product or investor performance. These rates do not account for performance risks, fees, expenses, or taxes associated with real investments. If these costs were included, the projected amounts would be lower, and the time needed to double the investment would be longer. Since the rate of return on investments fluctuates over time, the actual duration to double an investment's value cannot be predicted with certainty. Investing involves risks, including the potential loss of principal.

Here's how it works: Take the number 72 and divide it by the annual interest rate percentage of your investment. The result tells you the approximate number of years it will take for your money to double.

72 ÷ 1% = 72 years

If your interest rate is 1%, as shown above, it would take 72 years for $1 to turn into $2, which is a ridiculously long time! If you want your money to double faster so you can use it later in life for all the things you want for yourself, your family, and retirement, you'll need to do better than 1%.

Let's see how exciting things get as your rate of return increases...

Abracadabra!

72 ÷	
3%	24 years to double
6%	12 years to double
9%	8 years to double
12%	6 years to double

Can The Doubles Really Make That Big of a Difference?

Let's answer this question with a fun, hypothetical example using some of the cast of the book—Ashley, Tyler, Leo, Maria, and Hector (along with their future, retirement-aged selves). Together, they'll help us uncover the true power of the Rule of 72, which—as you now know—approximates how long it takes for money to double based on a given interest rate.

Each character starts with a $10,000 lump sum saved at age 19. For each, we'll apply increasing rates of return from 1% to 12% and calculate how many times their money doubles before they reach the retirement age of 67.[9] As we track their growing balances, the results will show just how dramatically small increases in interest rates can impact their final earnings.

1% gets Ashley to $16,000 with less than 1 double

Ashley kicks things off. Wanting safety and easy access to her money, she put her $10,000 in a savings account that gave her a 1% return. Let's apply our Rule of 72 formula: 72 ÷ 1% = 72 years to double. Yikes! By the time Ashley turns 67, her money hasn't even doubled once (aka gotten to $20,000).

Tyler was able to get a 3% interest rate. Let's see where he ended up...

3% gets Tyler to $40,000 with 2 doubles

With only 2 doubles, his results are better than Ashley's, but as you can see, 67-year-old Tyler is not very enthusiastic about his $10,000 only becoming $40,000.

At 3%, the growth still falls short of six figures. But we get there with Leo, who secures a 6% rate of return and 4 doubles. With his money doubling every 12 years, he's able to create a $160,000 nest egg for retirement.

6% gets Leo to $160,000 with 4 doubles

Now we're beginning to see the true power of exponential growth. As numbers double, the results seem almost unbelievable. Next up is Maria, who obtains a 9% rate of return for her $10,000, resulting in 6 doubles. By age 67, her $10,000 grows to an astonishing $640,000!

9% gets Maria to $640,000 with 6 doubles

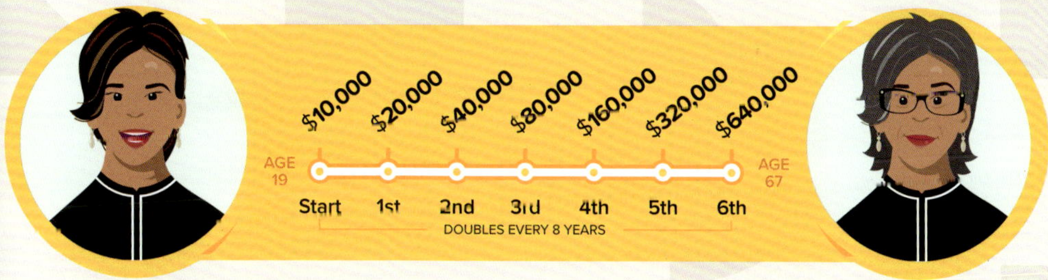

Finally—and for our grand finale—Hector shows us what a 12% rate of return yields. With 8 doubles (every 6 years), **his one time lump sum soars to $2,560,000!**

12% gets Hector to $2,560,000 with 8 doubles

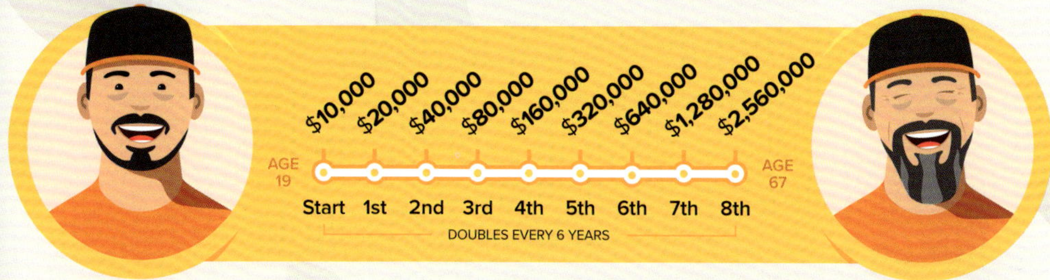

The Rule of 72 helps you estimate the growth trajectory of your savings. With only 4 more doubles than Leo at 6%, Hector earns **16 times** as much money!

What Would Your Older Self Tell You?

When Ashley was 19 years old, she parked a $10,000 lump sum in a money market account with a 1% return. It was low risk and gave her easy access to her money, but it will take about 72 years for her money to double. Unfortunately, Ashley didn't use the Rule of 72 to see that her money could double a lot faster with a higher interest rate.

Wouldn't it be great to hear from Ashley at 67—the Ashley who had to PAY LATER for her blunder almost five decades previous? What advice would she give her younger self? **Let's find out...**[9]

So, what can 'Mr. Boot Polish' do for me?

He'd use the Rule of 72 to show you how our money can double faster at higher rates of return within a variety of different types of financial vehicles. It would be clear to you that a money market account offering a 1% rate of return would grow our cash too slowly.

The bank told me the interest rate was pretty good for a money market account. They gave me a sucker afterwards.

It was root beer flavored, our fav—and I still feel like a dumb-dumb. Look at this chart, Ashley. Recently, the average rate of return for money market accounts was .34%,[10] which would double in about 212 years. You were lucky to get 1%—but it still means our cash has only grown to $16,000 by my age, which kinda sucks if I'm being honest. See the problem?

Account Type	Average[10]
Savings	0.15%
Money Market	0.34%

I do. 212 years is a long time. So is 72 years at the rate I got. Sorry, Old Ashley—your hair looks sick though.

Thanks—and let's go with 'Classic' Ashley. At 24, you have time to correct this mistake. Call 'Mr. Boot–'... I mean, call Tex and work with him to use the Rule of 72 to see how many doubles we can get. Let's do our research to look for higher rates of return like Maria and Hector did. It's time to ACT NOW. Get to it...

Recently, there was more than $12 trillion in money market and passbook savings accounts that earn, on average, 0.34% and 0.15%, respectively.[10,11]

If your money is held in a money market account earning just 0.34%, it would take around 212 years to double!

How much interest are you earning in YOUR bank account?

Great to hear, Leo. If you get stuck, try calling your bank or visiting a local branch.

The Rule of 72 Can Work Against You Too!

When you put your money in a money market or passbook savings account, the bank may use your funds to make loans to other customers. And recent data informs us that an average money market account doubles in about 212 years.

Check this—when you get a credit card, **you're borrowing money from the bank.** In this case, the bank is the one earning interest FROM YOU. If your money doubles in 212 years, how fast do you think THEIR money doubles?

Would you guess it's every 3.4 years?!

That's right. The average existing credit card interest rate is 21.37%.[12]

You get less than 1%. They get over 20%. Further support for the theory, the biggest buildings in any city are owned by banks and why they may not want financial literacy taught in schools.

Sucker anyone?

> **You do a personal audit, Ashley. It's not as hard as it sounds, and it could be worth thousands to you.**

Collect all your bank, retirement, and investment account statements, along with your credit card and loan statements. Calculate the impact of the Rule of 72 by applying it to your rates of return to determine how many doubles work in your favor and how many benefit your bank or lender. Use this insight to make adjustments—aim to increase the returns on your savings and reduce the interest rates or balances on your debts. This is a great opportunity to collaborate with your financial professional.

ACT NOW

- ☑ Memorize the Rule of 72 formula—it's simple!
- ☑ Use the Rule of 72 to evaluate how many doubles you'll get before opening any savings or investment account.
- ☑ Work with your financial professional to evaluate the current rates of return for all your accounts.

PAY LATER

- ☒ Dismiss the Rule of 72 as insignificant for your future.
- ☒ Make big decisions with your money without considering the rate that your money will double.
- ☒ Ignore the fact that you may have too much money sitting in a bank account with an interest rate that will take more than a lifetime for your money to double.

The 7
Money Milestones

1. FINANCIAL EDUCATION
2. PROPER PROTECTION
3. EMERGENCY FUND
4. DEBT MANAGEMENT
5. CASH FLOW
6. BUILD WEALTH
7. PROTECT WEALTH

The 7 Money Milestones

The 7 Money Milestones are your checklist for taking control of your money. Our lives change as we begin our career, start a family, acquire assets, change jobs, start businesses, experience health challenges, or lose loved ones. While each Milestone is important to consider and reassess wherever you are in life, some will be more important than others at different points on your path.

1 Financial Education

- Become financially literate
- Find a financial professional

2 Proper Protection

- Protect against loss of income
- Protect against loss of savings

3 Emergency Fund

- Save 3-6 months' income
- Prepare for unexpected expenses

4 Debt Management

- Change spending habits
- Strive to eliminate debt

5 Cash Flow

- Earn additional income
- Manage expenses

6 Build Wealth

- Try to avoid the impact of taxes, losses, and inflation
- Accumulate and grow assets for the future

7 Protect Wealth

- Create a will
- Guard your legacy

There is, TJ. The Milestones on the first page are short-term actions. The two at the top of this page are long-term actions.

Smart Tips For Starting Your Money Milestones Journey

The ACT NOW mindset we emphasize in this book applies directly to the 7 Money Milestones—it's all about building momentum. Taking action and staying consistent are what will help set you up for success as you work through each step. And here's the thing: the Milestones aren't something you're meant to tackle solo. Each one is designed to be navigated alongside a financial professional who can help you make informed decisions and stay on course.

Think of this as a partnership to help you move toward financial security and independence faster and with more confidence. Use these tips to make the most of every step you take!

The 7 Money Milestones are pivotal markers in your financial journey.

They represent the path to real world security and prosperity achievements, such as paying off debt, saving for retirement, purchasing a home, or investing in education.

Recognizing and celebrating these Milestones is crucial.

By setting and accomplishing these Milestones, you can systematically manage your finances, prepare for unforeseen expenses, and help ensure a comfortable lifestyle both now and in the future.

Financial educators guide students and clients through these steps.

In classrooms, web conferencing courses, and 1-on-1 sessions, financial educators help their students and clients make informed decisions that align with their goals and aspirations. Locate an educator near you to help you navigate the steps.

When plotting your financial roadmap, don't go it alone.

Working with a financial professional can help guide you in areas like debt management, investment strategies, and long-term planning.

Milestone 1

ACQUIRE A

Financial Education

Before we can navigate the financial landscape effectively, it's critical for all of us to gain a thorough understanding of money management principles. If you dedicate yourself to growing your financial education, you can move from inexperienced to proficient, and then from proficient to accomplished. It takes time and commitment—and the belief that this is not rocket science. It is a subject you can master, no matter how young you are.

Consider this book the beginning of your financial education. This book is part of TheMoneyBooks.com series. Each book in the series is specialized for a different demographic and offers the essential knowledge required to comprehend the intricacies of personal finance. Gaining financial knowledge is a foundational step—a comprehensive financial education arms you with the necessary tools to make informed decisions that will positively influence your future and the financial well-being of your family.

Get a Benchmark By Taking The Financial Literacy Quiz

Visit taketheflq.com which is created by the same people behind TheMoneyBooks to get your Financial Literacy Score and discover where you are currently with your financial literacy.

You'll be able to see where your strong and weak areas are which can inform you where to focus your educational efforts. And you'll be able to create a benchmark for the starting point of your financial literacy. As you progress with your education, you can take the quiz again to see how you've improved!

> **"Academic qualifications are important and so is financial education. They're both important and schools are forgetting one of them.**
>
> - ROBERT T. KIYOSAKI

Milestone 2

ENSURE

Proper Protection

Let's start at square one: what exactly is life insurance? It's pretty simple—it's insurance on your life. If you pass away, someone you've chosen (your 'beneficiary') will receive a specific amount of money.

But why would they need money after you're gone? Honestly, there are a lot of reasons. Think about it—what might you leave behind? Maybe debts, a mortgage, or a family that relies on you. Your beneficiary could use that money to take care of those things—and yes—even your funeral expenses. The truth is, in today's world, money keeps everything moving, even after we're gone.

Here's something a lot of young adults haven't thought about yet: the value of their income. If you have a family, they don't just depend on you—they depend on your paycheck. When you're no longer here, that income is gone too—not just this year's, but everything you would've earned in the years ahead. (Yes, this might sound a bit grim, but it's the easiest way to understand why life insurance matters.) Life insurance steps in to cover that 'lost earning potential,' ensuring your loved ones are financially secure if something ever happens to you.

**There's a few ways to estimate this, guys.
Let's check that out next. But to determine the right amount for you, work with your financial professional.**

"

You don't buy life insurance because you are going to die, but because those you love are going to live.

— DR. MARIUS BARNARD

(CARDIAC SURGEON AND FOUNDER OF CRITICAL ILLNESS INSURANCE)

"

It is a strange anomaly that men should be careful to insure their houses, their ships, their merchandise, and yet neglect to insure their lives—surely the most important of all to their families and more subject to loss.

— BENJAMIN FRANKLIN

How Much Life Insurance Do You Need?

It might be more than you expect, but don't freak out—there's good news. While you may need more life insurance than you realize, there's nearly a 50% chance you'll overestimate its cost.[13]

Just keep that in mind as you run your numbers.

Calculating how much life insurance you need will be based on a number of factors that should be determined with the help of your financial professional. However—for a quick estimation—here are a couple simple formulas to see what you might need.

SIMPLE FORMULA 1

The 10X METHOD

Aim for about 10 times your annual income.

Annual Income x 10 = Total Life Insurance Need

SIMPLE FORMULA 2

THE DIME METHOD

If you want a more customized estimate, use this method that adds up 4 key cost areas to calculate your life insurance need.

Debt *Credit cards, car loans, and personal loans*

Income *Annual income x 10*

Mortgage *Remaining balance on your home mortgage*

\+ **Education** *Estimate future education costs for your children*

Total Life Insurance Need

2 Basic Types of Insurance

Let's break it down. Life insurance comes in two main types: **Term Life Insurance**—and—**Permanent Life Insurance.**

Neither is inherently better than the other—it all depends on your unique circumstances. Factors like age, budget, coverage duration, financial goals, health, family and dependents, estate planning needs, and policy flexibility will determine which type is right for you. In some cases, you might even need a combination of both. That's why partnering with a financial professional is crucial to help you assess your needs and make an informed decision.

Let's take a look at both types...

Term Life Insurance

Term life insurance is just what it sounds like—coverage for a specific period of time—or 'term.' Its main advantage is that it's usually more affordable, thanks to the time limit on the policy.

The downside is that it's not an asset that grows over time—it's just an expense like car insurance. You pay a monthly premium, and if you need it, you benefit from the coverage. But if you don't use it—say, you don't get into an accident—you're relieved, but you won't get any money back.

Term life works the same way: if you pass away during the term, your beneficiary receives a payout. If you outlive the term, no payout occurs. You're glad you didn't need it, but ultimately, term life isn't an asset. It can provide peace of mind, helping to ensure that your loved ones are financially protected should something happen to you.

Take a look at the chart below. It shows how life typically moves from 'More Responsibility, Less Wealth; to 'More Wealth, Less Responsibility.' Early on, with less savings and more financial obligations (like loans, mortgages, and children), you need more life insurance. As your wealth grows and responsibilities decrease, your coverage needs shrink. Term life insurance is a great way to protect your loved ones during this early, high-responsibility stage.

The Financial X-Wave

of Decreasing Responsibility and Increasing Wealth

Permanent Life Insurance

Permanent life insurance, as the name suggests, lasts for your entire lifetime. In other words, it's a policy you keep for life, not just a term. The core benefit is that it provides continuous coverage, no matter what health changes occur.

It also allows you to build cash value within the policy, essentially creating an asset where your money grows over time. The cash value benefit includes a few advantageous features and options. For instance, the money grown in your account can offer tax advantages and protection from losses.

Another important option to mention regarding permanent life Insurance is that you can add a 'Long-Term Care' (LTC) rider to a permanent policy. A rider is an extra feature—an 'add on' if you will—and the LTC rider helps cover potential future costs like in-home care or nursing home expenses. Riders are available at an additional cost. Many people have witnessed the financial burden of caring for aging family members, so having LTC coverage as part of your permanent life insurance is a cost-effective way to prepare for these inevitable needs, compared to a standalone LTC policy.

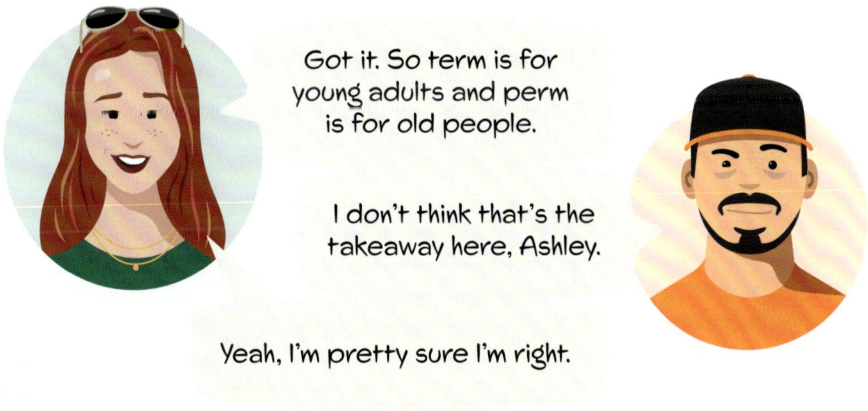

You might want to listen to Hector on this one, Ashley.

Here's a quick summary of the difference: Permanent life insurance provides lifelong coverage and builds cash value, while term life insurance only offers coverage for a specific period with no cash value. Permanent policies are more expensive due to the cash value component and lifetime protection.

Life Insurance is For The Next Generation Too

We're young, so it makes sense that many of us don't consider life insurance a priority yet—especially for those of us who don't have kids, a partner, or a mortgage to worry about yet. But here's the thing: getting life insurance in our 20's or 30's is actually one of the smartest financial moves we can make. The earlier we act, the more options and benefits we'll have in the future.

Here's why life insurance matters for you:

1. **Lock It In While You're Young and Healthy**
   When it comes to life insurance, your age and health play a huge role in determining your eligibility and cost. Right now, you're more likely to qualify easily because you're young and (hopefully) healthy. If you wait until later, health conditions could make it harder—or more expensive—to get covered.

2. **Save Money with Lower Premiums**
   Life insurance is far cheaper when you're young. Locking in a policy now means you'll pay lower premiums (a premium is the monthly cost paid to keep a life insurance policy active), saving you thousands in the long run. Even waiting five or ten years could mean higher premiums, and that's money you could be using for something else.

3. **Build a Financial Safety Net for Loved Ones**
   If something were to happen to you, your loved ones could still face financial obligations like co-signed student loans, car payments, or credit card debt. Having life insurance helps to ensure they won't be burdened with these costs. It's a way to protect those who've supported you.

4. **Use It as a Tool for Retirement**
   Life insurance can do more than just provide a payout to your beneficiaries. Certain policies can grow over time and be used as supplemental retirement income (supplemental retirement income is extra income beyond primary retirement sources, like Social Security or personal savings). By starting early, you can build this financial tool into your long-term strategy, giving you options when you need them most.

5. **Peace of Mind, With or Without Kids**
   You don't need dependents to benefit from life insurance. Having a policy provides peace of mind that your finances are in order no matter what happens. It's one less thing to worry about as you focus on building your career, traveling, or planning your future.

6 Cover Funeral Costs

Funeral expenses are higher than ever, averaging around $8,000.[14] Without life insurance, this cost could fall on your parents or close friends. A policy helps to ensure they're not left with the financial stress of saying goodbye.

Navigating life insurance might seem overwhelming, but it's simpler with the right guidance. A financial professional can help you:

- Determine whether term or permanent life insurance is better for your goals.
- Decide how much coverage you need.
- Find a policy that fits your budget and future plans.

Unlike other types of insurance, life insurance is about long-term thinking. It's not just protection for today—it's an investment in your future. By acting now, you're setting yourself up for financial stability and peace of mind down the road.

Good to hear that you're going to re-evaluate, Val. You're highlighting an important point that each person's needs can be unique, which is why we can't state enough how important it is to work with a financial professional.

Milestone 3

ESTABLISH AN

Emergency Fund

Even the most careful budgeter will eventually face an unexpected expense. Think about the three little pigs: the first two built their houses out of hay and sticks, and when the wolf showed up, they weren't ready. Don't make the same mistake—your emergency fund is like the brick house, built to handle whatever life throws at you.

An emergency fund is a stash of cash set aside specifically for life's surprises, like a flat tire, a medical bill, or an unexpected layoff. It's there to keep you on track financially, so you don't have to drain your savings, go into debt, or derail your long-term goals when the unexpected happens.

As a student, I don't have a lot of money. I work part-time in one of Hector's food trucks, but I make so little. Where do I get the cash to create an emergency fund?

That's OK, Zoey. Just save a little each month until you reach your goal.

The recommended goal is to have 3 to 6 months of your income in your emergency fund. This gives you precious breathing room in case of missed work, medical bills, property damage, broken appliances, surprise IRS fees—you name it. If you're currently living paycheck-to-paycheck, like many people are today,[15] your emergency fund could be the insulation that separates you from financial disaster.

As you work towards your 3-6 month emergency fund, start by making your first goal 2 weeks of pay. Then 1 month, then 2, until you reach your goal. With your emergency fund in place, you're no longer broke. Way to go!

THE 2 RULES OF AN

Emergency Fund

Rule #1

Keep in mind your emergency fund is **ONLY** for unexpected emergencies. Resist the temptation to use it for last minute birthday presents, much needed spa days, or irresistible Black Friday sales. It doesn't matter if it sits in your checking, savings, or a separate account—as long as it doesn't lure you to use it for anything but a true emergency.

Rule #2

If you need to use your emergency fund to fix a car, replace the fridge, or pay for braces, take the money and spend it. That's what it's for. Just make sure that afterwards you add back a little money every month until your emergency fund is full again.

Milestone 4

IMPLEMENT

Debt Management Strategies

What is the #1 objection we hear from those in early adulthood as to why they aren't sure they should start investing and saving for their future yet?

They think they should get rid of their debt first.

Balancing the desire to save for the future while managing student loans, credit card debt, or personal loans can feel overwhelming. It's a challenge many face, but the good news is that with the right approach, it's absolutely possible to work toward both goals simultaneously.

So how do you prioritize your financial decisions and future goals when you have existing debt?

Maybe your debt is in the form of student loans, maybe it's in credit cards, and/or maybe in the form of big adulting things like a mortgage or car payments. It is rare to find someone not in debt to be honest.

One at a time, let's break down these 4 most common types of debt in early adulthood:

1. Student Loan Debt
2. Credit Card Debt
3. Car Loan Debt
4. Home Mortgage Debt

LOL, TJ. That's a little dramatic. There's help for everyone in debt. Let's all learn more about how to avoid, manage, and reduce debt...

"A formal education will make you a living; self-education will make you a fortune.

— JIM ROHN
AMERICAN ENTREPRENEUR AND MOTIVATIONAL SPEAKER

Killer quote from Rohn. I graduated from one of the best industrial engineering schools in the country and never once learned how money works. I've never been in debt, but it's what I'm learning now on my own that will help me stay out of debt so I can focus throughout my life on protecting, saving, and building wealth.

I wasn't taught about money, but—for me—that's no excuse! Since it's my future, it's my responsibility to commit myself to my own financial education.

1 Student Loan Debt

Student loan debt often feels like a 'necessary evil' or even 'good debt,' especially since it's seen as the ticket to a better future. For older generations, life looked pretty straightforward: graduate high school, land a solid job, work there for decades, earn a pension, and retire. Sure, it sounds a little bleak when you think about retiring just a few years before passing away, but that was the reality for many.

For us, things are different. The high school goal wasn't just graduation—it was about getting the grades to make it into college. College was supposed to be where we figured out what we wanted to 'be when we grew up' and prepared for a job in that field. But that extra time spent earning a degree has shifted everything else in our lives.

We're getting married later, buying homes later, and starting families later—all milestones that impact our financial picture. And for those of us pursuing advanced degrees, like a master's or doctorate, these timelines are pushed back even further. It's a whole new reality for our generation, and student loans are often at the center of it.

This cultural shift in America began in the 1970's, when attending college transitioned from being a privilege or distinction to becoming the default next step after high school—even if the money wasn't there to cover it. Sure, some of us were fortunate enough to have parents or grandparents who saved or invested to pay for our tuition, but for many, taking out loans became the only option. Some of us even worked through college to cover tuition, housing, books, and other expenses, but that often wasn't enough to avoid debt entirely.

As a result, more and more 18–22 year-olds started their adult lives with significant debt, primarily from student loans.[16] If you're one of them, it's likely a choice you made to keep up with rising college costs and the pressure to stay competitive in today's job market. And you're far from alone: over 43 million people in the U.S. currently have federal student loans, contributing to a staggering $1.6 trillion (yes, trillion with a 'T'!) in outstanding debt.[17]

$1.6 Trillion

As of June 2024, Americans are carrying around $1.6 trillion in student loan debt—that's 42% more than just ten years ago. It makes sense when you think about it: more of us are going to college, and the cost of higher education just keeps climbing.[18]

– 5 –

Fascinating Facts[18]

ABOUT STUDENT LOAN DEBT

1. About 25% of U.S. adults under 40 are carrying student loan debt.
2. The typical bachelor's degree holder who borrowed owed between $20,000 and $24,999.
3. College graduates with student loans are more likely to report financial struggles compared to those without student debt.
4. College graduates with student loans generally have higher household incomes than those who didn't finish college.
5. Young college graduates with student loan debt are more likely than those without debt to say their education wasn't worth the cost.

Paying Back Your Student Loans After Graduation

When you finally get into your first 'grown up' job, which has been the finish line for so long, you typically also have to start paying back student loans. In many people's case, the amount you have to pay back each month can feel like a second rent payment! You're not just paying off the amount you borrowed—you're paying off the loan plus interest (remember, this is interest working against you—it's also how student loan companies make money).

Borrower Type	Student Loan Type	Interest Rate[19]
Undergraduate	Direct Subsidized & Unsubsidized	6.53%
Graduate & Professional	Direct Unsubsidized	8.08%
Parent, Graduate & Professional	PLUS	9.08%

Let's say your student loan interest rate is 6.5%, and you're considering an investment option with a potential return of 9%. In this scenario, the difference—2.5%—represents your potential net gain by investing rather than focusing solely on paying off your student loans early. That extra growth could go toward building your future savings. In some cases, it may make financial sense to invest instead of accelerating loan payments, but it's important to calculate your specific numbers and let the math guide your decision.

If your student loan interest rates are lower than the potential returns from investments, you might want to consider investing some of your extra funds.

If your student loan interest rates are higher than the potential returns from investments, paying down your loan principal could be a smart choice.

Consult with your financial professional to determine the best approach for your situation.

Is Refinancing Your Student Loan Right For You?

Refinancing your student loans is an option worth considering! By lowering your interest rate, even by a few percentage points, you can significantly reduce the total interest you pay over time. This could also free up more room in your budget, allowing you to start saving for your future. There are numerous student loan calculators that you can find online that can help you explore different scenarios and understand how refinancing might impact your finances.

Grab your financial professional and experiment with the numbers to explore if refinancing could be a smart move for you!

When considering a student loan refinancing company, here are some quick tips to make sure the company is reputable:

1. **Licensing & Accreditation**
   Verify the company on websites like the Better Business Bureau (BBB) or Consumer Financial Protection Bureau (CFPB).

2. **Transparency**
   Reputable companies clearly disclose terms and fees upfront, without hidden costs. Avoid companies that charge fees for basic services like loan applications or early repayment.

3. **Reviews and Complaints**
   Read reviews on the BBB and CFPB. Look for any recurring complaints about scams, poor service, or unfulfilled promises.

4. **Customer Service**
   Look for clear channels of communication and how responsive they are to inquiries or issues.

5. **Avoid High-Pressure Sales Tactics**
   Legitimate companies do not use aggressive tactics to get you to sign up quickly or rush you into making decisions.

6. **Research Loan Types and Terms**
   Check if they offer fixed rates, which are typically safer, versus variable rates.[20]

2 Credit Card Debt

Many of us grew up hearing "don't get into credit card debt—it's a really harmful type of debt." Unfortunately, many of us haven't listened. Credit card debt held by Millennials and Gen-Z is steeply on the rise since 2021, as you can see in the chart below.

Average Credit Card Debt by Generation, 2012–2024[21]

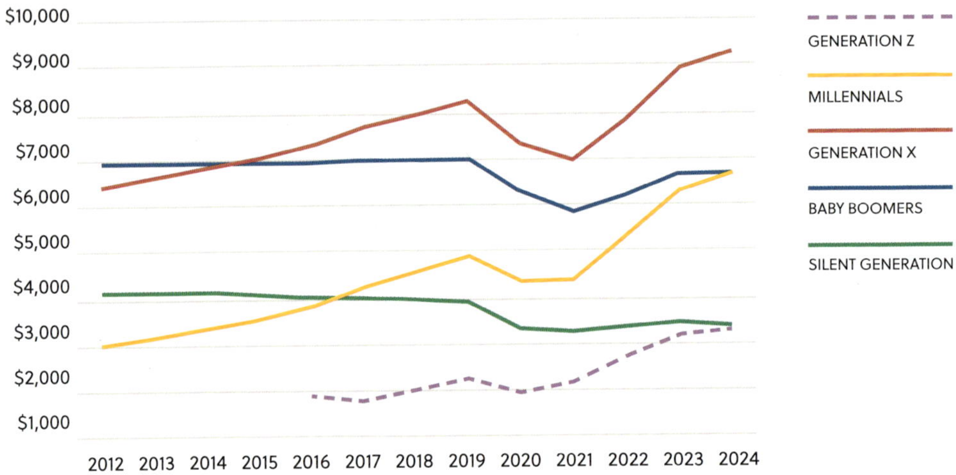

Credit card debt can be one of the hardest types to escape once you're in it.

So why do so many of us end up here?

Often, it's because we use debt to keep up with a lifestyle that exceeds our income, instead of waiting until we can afford it. For instance, if someone earns $60,000 but needs $72,000 to cover all their expenses—both wants and needs—a credit card can fill that $12,000 gap.

We convince ourselves we'll soon earn more and pay it off, whether through a promotion or a side hustle. But $12,000 is like spending an extra $1,000 a month, and soon, small purchases like groceries or unexpected expenses—like a new tire or an impulse buy—start adding up, pushing the debt higher.

It's The Interest Rates That Kill Us

Credit card companies know exactly what they are doing. They know that you don't want to wait until you are making $1,000 extra a month to increase your lifestyle. They know you want what you want—and you want it right now.

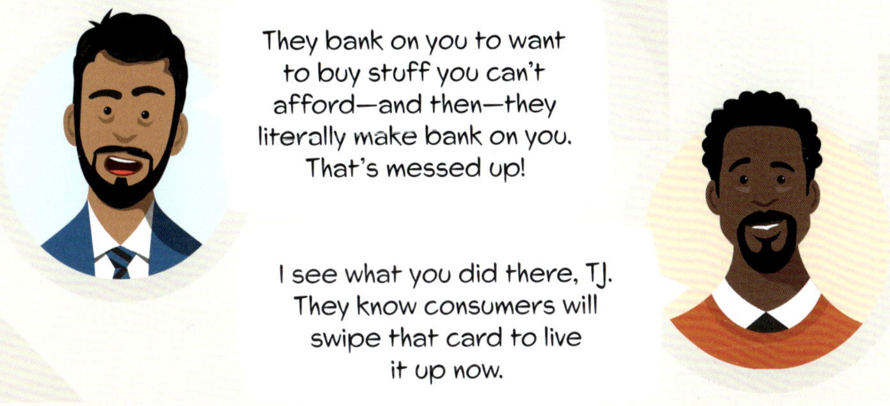

The typical interest rate for credit cards in America is 21.37%.[12]

You know how the Rule of 72 math works—their money is doubling every 3 years, while you're living life and digging yourself deeper into credit card debt. So, how do you get out of this hole?

There are several approaches, but we recommend the 'Snowball Method.' With this strategy, you start by paying off the card with the lowest balance. Once it's cleared, you move on to the next one. The key is the quick win—paying off that first card gives you motivation and shows the results of your effort. After clearing the first card, you apply the amount you were paying towards it to the next card.

Make it your mission to put every penny you can towards paying off those cards. Stay focused and keep the momentum going!

Also remember: As you're paying down your debt with the Snowball Method, avoid buying things with your credit card(s). This may seem obvious, but you'd be surprised how many people increase their debt while trying to pay it down.

Credit Scores—A Brief Overview

This is one of those topics where you know it's important and feel like you're supposed to have 'a good one,' but you might not know much beyond that. We've heard the question countless times: "How do I even know if I have one?"

Here's the thing: most people get their first credit card to 'establish credit.' In simple terms, this means you start using credit so lenders (the people or companies who lend money) can assess how reliable you are at paying it back.

And how do they measure that reliability? Through your credit score. Think of it as a grade for your financial trustworthiness. Your score ranges from 300 to 850, with higher scores indicating better creditworthiness.

Credit Score Breakdown by FICO[22]

Below 580: Poor

580 to 669: Fair

670 to 739: Good

740 to 799: Very Good

800 and above: Exceptional

Calculate Your Debt-to-Credit Ratio

You know how your credit card has a limit? Let's say you have two cards: Card A with an $8,000 limit and Card B with a $12,000 limit. Together, your 'total available credit' is $20,000. Now, if you have a $2,000 balance on Card A and a $5,000 balance on Card B, your total credit card debt is $7,000.

Your debt-to-credit ratio is calculated by dividing your total debt ($7,000) by your total credit ($20,000), which equals 0.35, or 35%. (Cue your math teacher saying, "Move the decimal two places to find the percentage!") Ideally, you should keep this ratio below 30% to maintain a healthy credit score. In this example, lowering debt closer to $6,000 (30% of $20,000) would likely improve your credit score.

Why does this matter? A good credit score is essential for renting an apartment, buying a car, securing a mortgage, opening new credit cards, setting up some utilities or cell phone plans, starting a business, and even determining insurance premiums in certain states.

Your credit score tells lenders and landlords how reliable you are at repaying debts—essentially how financially responsible you are. It also directly impacts the interest rates you receive: higher scores typically mean lower rates, while lower scores lead to higher costs over time.

You can check on your credit score any time by going to:
annualcreditreport.com

You get one free report each year from each of the three credit bureaus. That means you could download one every four months, or two every 6 months, or all three at one time annually. We recommend putting a reminder in your phone so you don't forget, whatever frequency you choose.

3 Car Loan Debt

A car loan allows you to borrow money to buy a car, which you repay over time, typically over 3 to 7 years. Like any loan, it includes interest—the cost of borrowing money.

Here's the key point: A car is not generally considered an investment because cars lose value over time. A new car can depreciate by 20-30% in its first year alone, and will be worth about 40% what you paid in 5 years.[23]

That said, a car is a necessity for many people, so a car loan isn't viewed as 'bad debt'—like most credit card debt. Instead, it's considered a 'neutral' type of debt—not inherently good or bad, but something to approach with careful planning.

The key to making a good purchase is to do your research. Consider:

- Budget *(includes car price, insurance, taxes, and maintenance cost)*
- Research reliability ratings, resale value, and reviews from other owners
- Fuel efficiency—how much do you drive? How many times will you have to fill up at the pump each month? Do you prefer a gas or electric powered car?
- Safety features of course!
- Manufacturer's warranty *(The car manufacturer promises to repair or replace certain parts of the vehicle for free if they fail due to defects in materials or workmanship within a specified period.)*
- Financing options if applicable *(Shop for the best rate, meaning sometimes a credit union can offer you a better rate than the dealership... or the dealership sometimes can offer you a better rate than the bank.)*
- The long-term—will your family size change? Will you need more cargo space?
- Test drive if you can—behind the wheel *is* a different experience than a 360-degree walkthrough online
- Negotiating—research fair market value so you can be prepared to have discussions

Three Car Loan Tips For Best Results

There's a bit to learn about buying a car if you want to have the best purchasing experience. Doing online research can feel overwhelming, with so much information to sift through. A simpler option? Reach out to someone you trust who knows a lot about cars and car buying. Sitting down with them over coffee to pick their brain can help cut through the noise. Start by discussing these three key tips...

1. **Know The Total Loan Amount**

   Don't just focus on the monthly payment—look at the total loan amount, including interest, to understand the full cost of financing the car.

2. **Increase Your Down Payment**

   A larger down payment reduces the amount you need to borrow and can lower your monthly payments. It can also help you avoid being 'upside-down' on your loan, where you owe more than the car is worth.

3. **Get Answers to Your Questions—All of Them!**

   Don't be intimidated—go in prepared! Write down your questions before visiting the dealership, and take notes throughout the process. Don't hesitate to ask for clarification and make sure every question is answered before making any decisions.

4 Home Mortgage Debt

We won't dive too deep into this type of debt, but since it becomes a part of early adulthood for many, let's cover the highlights.

Buying a home with a mortgage (essentially a loan on a physical property) is generally considered good debt. Why? Because when managed responsibly, it can positively impact your financial health. Residential properties that you purchase—like a house, townhouse, or condo—have the capacity to increase in value.

With a mortgage, you're building equity, which means you're investing in an asset. Over time, as that property may appreciate in value, your net worth can increase. Essentially, owning a home is an investment in real estate (look at you!) and is considered a long-term investment. It's also a long-term commitment, with common loan terms like the 30-year mortgage giving you decades to repay the debt.

Mortgage interest rates tend to be lower than other types of loans, and fixed-rate mortgages (where your rate stays the same for the entire term) provide predictability, making it easier to budget your payments over the life of the loan.

Should you pay extra toward your mortgage to pay it off faster than 30 years? It depends. Like student loans, mortgage interest rates are often lower than the potential returns you could earn by investing that extra money. Crunch the numbers with your financial professional and a mortgage calculator to decide what makes the most sense for your situation.

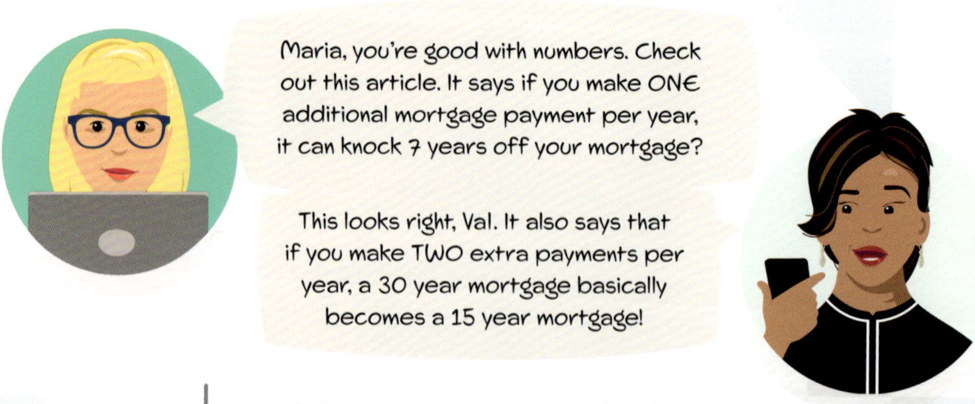

Your information is correct, ladies. With money, you just have to let the math guide you.

In the U.S., there are also potential tax benefits that come with homeownership. When you're ready to take this step, it's worth doing a quick search to learn about the most up-to-date benefits for that tax year.

Buying your first home is a huge step! Here is a little extra guidance to help make it way less stressful. You're going to do great!

6 Essential Guidelines for First-Time Home Buyers

1. **Start Saving for Your Down Payment ASAP**
   Saving for a down payment can feel overwhelming, but starting early makes a huge difference! Down payments usually range from 3% to 20% of the home price, depending on the loan.

2. **Know How Much Home You Can Afford**
   Be real about your budget! It's not just the mortgage—you'll also need to factor in property taxes, insurance, utilities, and maintenance. Lenders will tell you the max you qualify for, but go with what feels comfortable for your lifestyle.

3. **Explore Different Mortgage Options**
   There are a ton of loan options out there, like conventional, FHA, or VA loans. Each one has its own perks and quirks. Talk to a loan officer who can help you figure out what works best for you and your situation—it's worth asking a million questions!

4. **Get Pre-Approved Before House Hunting**
   Getting pre-approved means a lender has already reviewed your finances and is ready to give you a loan. Not only does this help you know your budget, but sellers LOVE it because it shows you're serious. Bonus points in competitive markets! (Keep in mind that the loan amount you get approved for may be higher than what your budget can actually bear.)

5. **Don't Forget About Closing Costs and Extra Expenses**
   Heads up—closing costs can sneak up on you! They're usually 2-5% of the home price and cover stuff like appraisals, title fees, and taxes. Make sure you budget for these alongside your down payment so you're not caught off guard.

6. **Check Out First-Time Homebuyer Assistance Programs**
   So many programs are out there to help first-timers with down payments and closing costs. Check out FHA grants, USDA loans, or state-specific programs. A little research here could save thousands.

A Conversation

WITH TJ, TYLER, AND HECTOR

My first question is, why did you take on so much debt if you can't afford it?
I used to make enough to cover it all but then I had to switch jobs and now I'm earning a lot less. Every month I'm overspending by hundreds.
My wife and I follow the 28/36 rule. Basically, you spend no more than 28% of your income on housing costs, including your mortgage, and no more than 36% on housing combined with other debts—like car loans, credit cards, or student loans.
They break it down on investopedia.com—just search for 'What Is a Reasonable Amount of Debt?'
That's good for the future, Hector—but it doesn't really help him now.
TJ, what can you downsize, dump, bump, or split?
Um, I guess I could sell the Tesla and get a used car. I could get a roommate to help cover some of the mortgage payment. And I may be able to save some by refinancing my student loans. Stinks, but I'd be in the positive again.
LET'S GO! And pay as much as you can on those credit cards every month until you hit zero. You gotta face this like it's WAR!
Or... like it's a game.
Thanks, guys! You really have to protect your cash flow. I wish there was a chapter on that topic...

Milestone 5

INCREASE YOUR

Cash Flow

Cash flow is the money you have available to spend, save, or invest. Once you've built a solid financial foundation—like an emergency fund and a smart debt strategy—you can shift your focus to growing your cash flow. It's a powerful tool for paying off debt faster and building your savings.

There's no secret formula or magic trick to boost your cash flow, but with some effort and discipline, there are proven strategies you can use to make it happen.

In this chapter, we'll focus on two key areas where almost anyone, with the right guidance, can increase their cash flow.

These 2 focus areas are:

Budgeting Money

Budgeting might not sound like fun at first, but it's a habit you'll be thankful for. It helps you spot wasted money, save more, and take control of your finances—all while boosting your peace of mind! Companies don't operate without budgets. Neither should your household.

Earning Money

Income, your job, and extra earning opportunities have many moving parts. If you're serious about saving more and spending less, there may be simple ways to boost your income and keep more of what you earn. Let's explore!

Budgeting Money

"

Do not save what is left after spending; instead spend what is left after saving.

— WARREN BUFFETT

First, we encourage you to think about budgeting a little differently—deciding where your money will go before you spend it can make a huge difference. Studies show that people who budget are happier, less anxious, make fewer impulse purchases, and feel more confident about their future.[24]

Maybe there's something to this whole budgeting and debt management thing after all. Creating a clear visual of your financial situation can be empowering because it helps you truly understand your numbers. Don't be afraid to experiment with different tools until you find one that feels right for you. (We'll dive into some of those options shortly.)

If sticking to a budgeting tool feels like a struggle, try committing to it for just three months. That's about how long it takes for spending patterns to emerge, and this information can be incredibly valuable.[25] Once you've got a handle on your financial flow, you might decide to stop using the tool—or keep it handy to get back on track if things start to slip again.

But who knows? After 90 days of budgeting, you might love the sense of financial security and peace of mind so much that you decide to stick with it for the long haul!

Getting Started With a Simple T-Chart

So, you're ready to start budgeting—amazing! Whether you're making it a long-term habit or just trying it for a few months, tracking your spending is the first step. It'll help you understand where your money is going, like housing, transportation, groceries, dining out, and fun expenses. Track every single dollar you spend—this is SO key to getting a clear picture of your finances.

No matter what budgeting tool you choose, we suggest starting with a simple T-chart. It's the easiest way to create a budget because it visually breaks down your cash flow—showing how much money is coming in (income) and how much is going out (expenses) each month. It's a great way to build awareness and take control!

My Budget

Income	Expenses
Main Job	Rent/Mortgage
Side Hustle	Transportation
	Food/Groceries
Total = $XX	Utilities
	Internet/Phone
	Miscellaneous

Options to Manage Your Day-to-Day Budget

This exercise is a real eye-opener for many people! We've heard from so many people who have told us how life-changing it is. They often say, "This is so easy—why didn't I do this years ago? I've just been blindly earning and spending my paycheck!"

Once you've completed your T-chart, congratulations—you've officially started budgeting! Give yourself a round of applause.

Now, to keep up the momentum and make budgeting a consistent habit, it's time to choose the right tool for managing your day-to-day budget.

Here are a couple of great options:

- **Pen and Paper (or a Simple Spreadsheet)**

If you're all about keeping things straightforward, a handwritten budgeting journal or a basic spreadsheet might be your best bet. This approach is perfect for those who prefer simplicity and want something easy to maintain. If you're unsure where to start, you can find great budgeting templates on Etsy, Google Drive, or Excel.

- **Use a Budgeting App**

If you love tech and want your budget at your fingertips, a budgeting app could be the way to go. Start by searching online for 'best budgeting apps' and read reviews to find one that suits your needs. For example, if tracking debt is your focus, look for apps with strong debt management features.

When choosing, think about compatibility with your devices and how the app fits your lifestyle. Apps that work on both a phone and browser are great because they offer flexibility. A phone app lets you check your budget on the go (like when you're about to walk into the grocery store), while a browser version is perfect for monthly check-ins, making adjustments, and spotting trends.

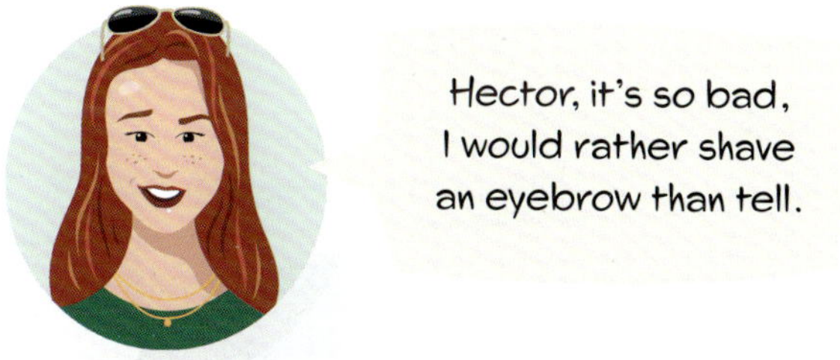

Use an Envelope System

There is also something called the cash-stuffing envelope system. This is a little 'old school,' but has recently gained renewed traction due to social media. Basically you keep a pre-decided amount of cash in an envelope for each category of expenses—a grocery envelope, a gas envelope, etc.

For example, if you have $100 cash in your gas envelope, once you spend $100 for the month, you are quite literally out of gas money. Now you could grab a little extra from the grocery envelope if needed, but of course that means you have less cash available for groceries.

The one thing we don't love about this system is that when cash is in an envelope, it isn't growing with interest. If you're only doing this system for 90 days as a way to inspire financial change in your life, we think that is wonderful! This method just may not be sustainable for a long period of time if you really want to maximize your money's potential.

Reverse Budget

As you start using your budgeting tool, we recommend keeping a concept called the 'reverse budget' in mind. This is all about paying yourself first, which we've previously touched on. The idea is to prioritize savings, then cover your needs, and finally, your wants. Many people already do this without even realizing it—like when you automatically contribute to your 401(k) from each paycheck.

But reverse budgeting is more of a mindset than a strategy. You've worked hard for your money, and it can be discouraging to watch your bank balance grow nicely on payday, only to see it disappear as bills get paid. Paying yourself first gives you control over your finances by ensuring you prioritize your future before anything else. By doing this, you can make intentional choices about how much you want to save before covering your needs and wants.

Pay yourself first.

– REVERSE BUDGET MINDEST

We get it—many people want specific, step-by-step advice, like "tell me exactly how much to put where!" That's where the 50/30/20 rule comes in. This means dividing your income into 50% needs, 30% wants and 20% savings. This helps you balance everyone's natural desire to live fully and enjoy life now, but also make smart savings decisions for your future self.

It's a simple guideline for dividing your income:

50/30/20 Rule

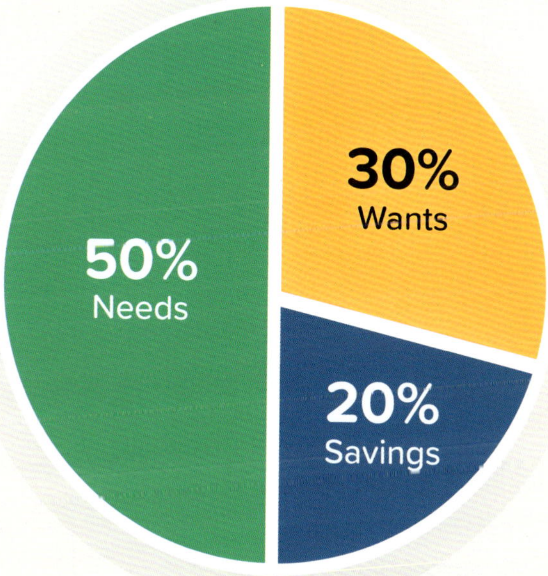

Time to test drive your budget! Identify which expenses are needs vs. wants and figure out what you're willing to cut. Prioritize spending categories—maybe you can drop some streaming services, switch phone plans, or save by packing lunch instead of ordering Uber Eats. Look for areas to reduce, replace, or remove entirely. For example, if you are paying for apps you're not using, reallocate those unnecessary expenses to pay off debt or boost your savings.

Find Help with Budgeting

We want to be sure to do our due diligence by letting you know: if you are looking for free counseling because you feel like you really can't do this yourself, there are resources available...

National Foundation for Credit Counseling (nfcc.org)

– AND –

Financial Counseling Association of America (fcaa.org)

We highly recommend trying to work with a financial professional first—which may be the person who gifted you this book!

Keep going—you can do this! We believe in you!

Earning Money

> **It's simple arithmetic: Your income can grow only to the extent that you do.**
>
> – T. HARV EKER

There are many ways to earn income, with the most common being as an employee or an entrepreneur. While you may already be familiar with much of what we'll cover, it's important to consider all the advantages of each path. This will help you assess whether your current way of earning income is truly the right fit for you.

Being an Employee

This might be obvious but, if you receive a W-2 at your job come tax season, you're an employee. Your employer could be a large Fortune 500 company or a small local business, a long-established, multi-generational company, or a brand-new startup. They might employ thousands of people or just a handful. Regardless of the size or type of the organization, as an employee, you'll enjoy certain benefits and responsibilities.

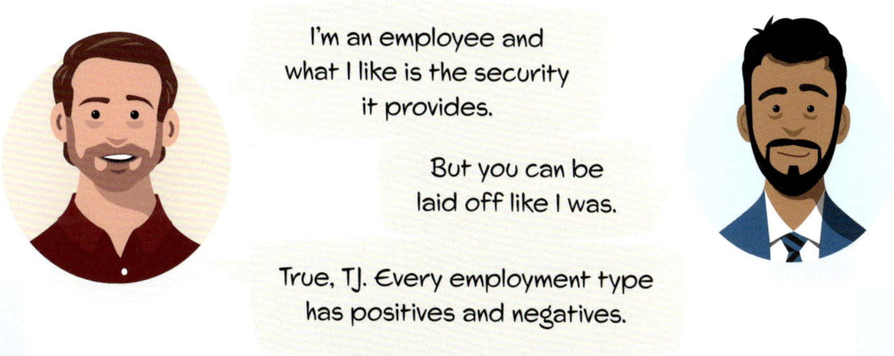

The Advantages of Having a Regular Job

A job essentially means you've agreed to exchange your time and expertise for money by performing specific duties. Along with your paycheck, many jobs come with additional perks, such as health insurance, retirement options like a 401(k) or 403(b), paid time off, and sometimes even stock options or personal benefits like cell phone reimbursement.

You also gain the stability of a consistent paycheck, simplified taxes thanks to automatic withholdings, and job security—especially with established companies. These benefits can significantly contribute to your financial stability and overall peace of mind.

But there are other, less-talked-about advantages worth considering:

- **Professional Development**
  Many employers invest in their employees' growth by covering costs for further education, training, or certifications. These opportunities not only enhance your skills but also boost your career. Networking within your company or industry can also open doors for future advancement.

- **Social Security and Medicare Contributions**
  Each paycheck includes contributions to these programs, ensuring your eligibility for important benefits down the road. Government employees should check to see if their employer participates in these programs.

- **Easier Access to Credit**
  A consistent income can make it simpler to qualify for major financial milestones, like getting a mortgage or a car loan.

- **Legal Protections**
  As a W-2 employee, you may be protected by labor laws that safeguard against discrimination and ensure rights like minimum wage, overtime pay, and workplace safety.

- **Predictable Hours**
  Having set work hours can provide structure to your week, making it easier to plan your personal time and responsibilities.

All these factors combine to make being an employee a potentially valuable and fulfilling path, depending on your goals and priorities.

One of the most common questions we get about employee benefits concerns retirement options offered by employers.

For example, if your employer offers a 401(k) or 403(b) plan, you need to know what these are and how they work. Simply put, they're retirement savings accounts.

Here's how they benefit both you and your employer:

For the employer: They get a tax deduction for offering these plans, which incentivizes them to provide retirement savings options to their employees.

For you: You can contribute a portion of your paycheck directly into the account, making it an easy way to save for your future. This contribution is taken from your gross pay (your salary before any deductions), which reduces your taxable income. As a result, you'll pay less in income taxes now while saving for retirement.

Quick vocab refresher...

Gross pay: Your total earnings before deductions like taxes and retirement contributions.

Net pay: What's left after all deductions—including taxes—that are taken out of your paycheck.

By participating in a 401(k) or 403(b) plan, you're not just saving for retirement—you're also lowering your taxable income in the short-term!

Here's a simple way to remember this:

Gross Pay = The Full Amount	Net Pay = What You Keep
▪ This is your total pay. ▪ Think of it as the 'Gross' total, like the 'gross weight' of something, which includes everything.	▪ What's left after deductions. ▪ Think like catching fish in a 'net'—you only keep what you catch (or take home). So, net pay is your 'take-home pay.'

How to Handle Employer Matching Contributions

What should you consider or ask yourself before deciding whether to participate in your employer's retirement plan? One of the most critical factors is: Does your company offer matching contributions?

So, what is matching? It's when your company matches a percentage of the money you contribute to your retirement account. For example, if you contribute 3% of your salary, your company might match that same 3%, essentially doubling your contribution. Some companies cap their match at a specific percentage, like 4%.

Here's how a 4% match would work:

- **You put in 3%, the company matches 3%**
- **You put in 4%, the company matches 4%**
- **You put in 5%, the company still only matches up to their cap of 4%**

Think of matching as a gift from your employer—free money that helps you build your future! Who wouldn't love that? Plus, your 401(k) or 403(b) grows tax-deferred, meaning you won't pay taxes as your balance increases. That gives your money even more room to grow, letting you take full advantage of the magic of compound interest! It's one of the smartest ways to make your savings work for you.

Now, everyone's situation is unique, but here are a few things to discuss with your financial professional (they can help you choose a direction):

- Since the menu of investment options is limited to those selected by your employer, do you only want to contribute enough to maximize their match and then explore other investment or savings options that might better suit your goals?
- If your plan allows, do you want your 401(k) contributions to be Traditional or Roth contributions? You will need to consider the tax implications of each.

Do you see where we're going with this? Don't worry if you're still wrapping your head around some of these concepts. In the next chapter, we'll dive deeper into taxes and how they interact with your retirement savings, so stay tuned—it's all going to make more sense soon!

Being an Entrepreneur

Entrepreneurship is a whole different game. It often starts with a simple idea—an innovative way to solve an everyday problem. Unlike the structure of a traditional 9-to-5, there's no boss to decide when you're ready for a promotion or a raise, and no set age limit for starting out. You don't need a huge investment or decades of experience to get started. What you do need is the ability to observe the world, spot opportunities to make things easier, more affordable, or more enjoyable, and then take action to build a business around those opportunities.

In today's world, launching a business has never been easier, thanks to the internet. You can set up a website, start advertising, and get things rolling in no time.

Have you ever imagined getting paid to do something you truly love? Once you begin dreaming about the possibilities, you'll start to see the world differently—full of challenges that are just waiting for innovative solutions. Maybe it's helping busy families with everyday tasks, creating sustainable products, or offering valuable services in your community. The opportunities are endless, and the rewards can be both financial and deeply fulfilling.

Hector, you have a food truck empire and I run my own CPA business. It's such a challenge, especially getting it started from scratch. What tips would you give to someone considering entrepreneurship?

You have to work hard, be self-driven, and get as much help as you can. But it is so worth it. I LOVE BEING MY OWN BOSS! I love the flexibility and freedom to do things my way.

On another note, any clue what Ashley's side gig is?

Yeah, I know. But she told me not to tell you. I think her job is really fun...

Is Entrepreneurship Right For You?

When considering if entrepreneurship is the right path for you, here are some things to think about:

Freedom

Make your own decisions, your own schedule, and feel a sense of independence. Creative freedom is included in terms of building something that reflects your vision and values.

Income Potential

Uncertainty often goes hand-in-hand with starting a business, but you also have the potential to earn significantly more than a salaried person, especially if the business succeeds and scales.

Flexibility and Work-Life Balance

You choose your daily schedule, meaning you work when you want to work and don't work when you don't want to work. Especially if you have a family and children, this can be an extremely valuable and motivating factor.

The Hidden Rewards of Entrepreneurship

There are some benefits of entrepreneurship that don't get discussed as often, and one of the most impactful is personal growth and development. Starting and running a business pushes you to learn and adapt constantly. You'll likely wear many 'hats,' which can strengthen your resilience, leadership, and problem-solving skills in ways few other experiences can.

Another significant benefit is the opportunity to build equity. By creating and growing a business, you're not just earning income—you're building an asset. Over time, this asset could become something valuable enough to sell for a substantial profit, giving you a long-term financial advantage.

Entrepreneurship also provides a unique form of job security. When you work for yourself, you don't have to worry about being laid off or fired. While it's true that some businesses fail, being your own boss gives you control over how to adapt your business to changing market conditions, providing a sense of stability that's hard to replicate elsewhere.

Ultimately, entrepreneurship is about more than just making money—it's about creating value. It's a chance to turn ideas into reality, solve problems for others, and take control of your future.

Take a look at your surroundings and consider: What problems can you solve? What opportunities can you seize? Don't hesitate to take that first step. With determination, creativity, and a problem-solving mindset, you already have the tools to make a difference—and to build wealth along the way.

My food trucks provide sandwiches with 100% organic ingredients. People wanted healthy options instead of just fried comfort food at school events and city concerts. What problem did you solve, Amiga?

¡Tus camiones de comida son geniales! Your food trucks rock, Señor Hector. I knew so many women who wanted a female CPA. So, I started a CPA firm for women only. I think you have to make sure the need is real—you test it with your actual clients and customers. And, there are some cool tax breaks available for business owners.

Side Gigs

Many Millennials and Gen-Zers are looking for ways to supplement their primary income by taking advantage of off-hours and filling gaps of time. It's one of the reasons the 'gig economy' has exploded over the past decade.

The possibilities for side gigs are practically endless. You could tutor math, babysit, or offer handyman services in your community. You might start an online business, like an Etsy shop, or offer skills like web or graphic design on the side. Maybe you've thought about starting a wedding planning service or a home organization business. Whatever your skills, hobbies, or interests, chances are there's a way to monetize them.

But here's a bit of tough love: if you know you need to earn more money and haven't taken steps to start a side gig, ask yourself—why not? What's holding you back? Sometimes, taking that first step is all it takes to unlock new opportunities and move closer to your financial goals.

Be honest with yourself. Do you genuinely not have the time to start a side gig, or are you spending a few hours a day watching Netflix or scrolling through your phone? No judgment from us—we're guilty of it too! But here's the reality: you are the product of your choices. Doing nothing is a choice. And more often than not, it's the small decisions and habits that add up over time and make a big difference.

For instance, if you spent just one hour each evening working on your side gig, that's seven hours by the end of the week—around 30 hours by the end of the month. That's almost a full workweek of extra effort every month! Now, imagine where your business could be today if you'd dedicated 30 hours to it last month.

Popular Side Gig Categories

The most popular side gig categories often reflect flexibility, low start-up costs, and the ability to use existing skills.

Freelancing and Online Services

- Writing, editing, or proofreading
- Graphic design or web design
- Social media management
- Programming or software development
- Virtual assistance

Selling Products Online

- Handmade crafts (e.g., on Etsy)
- Reselling items (e.g., through eBay, Poshmark, or Mercari)
- Dropshipping or print-on-demand businesses
- Digital products (e.g., templates, courses, or eBooks)

Sharing Economy Platforms

- Driving for Uber or Lyft
- Delivering for services like DoorDash, Instacart, or Uber Eats
- Renting out property or space on Airbnb
- Renting personal items (e.g., cars through Turo or equipment through Fat Llama)

Teaching and Tutoring

- Online tutoring (e.g., VIPKid, Wyzant)
- Teaching a skill or hobby (e.g., music lessons, fitness coaching)
- Creating and selling online courses (e.g., through Udemy or Teachable)

Home and Personal Services

- Babysitting or pet sitting (e.g., Care.com or Rover)
- Cleaning or organizing homes
- Lawn care, gardening, or handyman services
- Event planning or photography

Content Creation

- Blogging or vlogging (YouTube, Medium, Substack, etc.)
- Podcasting
- Becoming an influencer or affiliate marketer

Artistic and Creative Gigs

- Selling artwork, photography, or crafts
- Writing books or self-publishing
- Performing music or acting

Specialized Consulting or Coaching

- Career coaching or resume building
- Financial guidance or budgeting help
- Health and wellness coaching

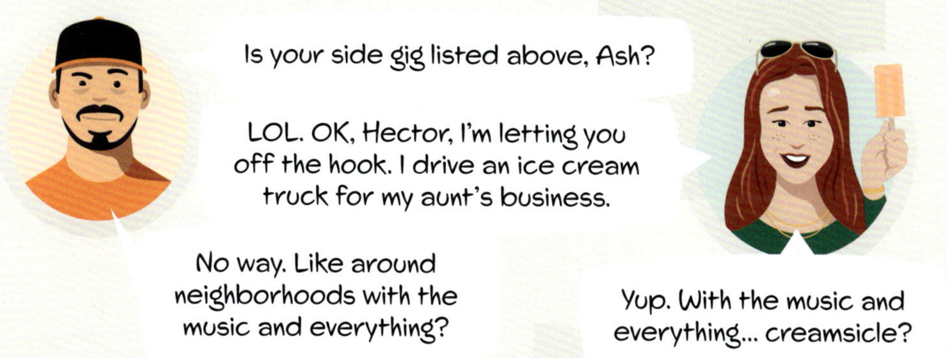

Milestone 6

ACCELERATE

Wealth Building

No matter how young you are or where your current financial situation stands, prioritizing wealth accumulation now is a game-changer. Seriously, this is one of those things your future self will be so thankful for. We've talked about this over and over in this book, but it's worth repeating—time is one of the greatest assets you'll ever have. And guess what? If you're 18, 23, or even 27, you've got a lot of time on your side. That's why now is the perfect time to start building wealth, even if it feels like you're starting small.

Think back to the chapters on the Power of Compound Interest and the Rule of 72. You know how money grows when you invest it wisely and let it work its magic over time. This isn't just theory—it's the key to building your financial future. With this Milestone, we're setting the foundation for what's to come: building wealth so we can create the financial security and independence we all want for our future selves.

But this isn't just about 'money' in a cold, boring sense. It's about so much more—like having the peace of mind that comes from knowing you're covered if life throws you a curveball. It's about enjoying a fulfilling lifestyle, whether that means traveling the world, starting a business, or just being able to say yes to opportunities without stressing over every penny. And let's not forget one of the best rewards of wealth: being able to give back to the people and causes you care about.

So, where do you even start?

First, take a deep breath. You don't need to have it all figured out right this second. The key is to start small and stay consistent. We're not here to recommend specific financial products (that's a conversation for you and your financial professional), but we are here to talk about the principles that can guide your wealth-building journey.

Start With The Basics

The key is to ACT NOW—because waiting never does us any favors. You don't need to be making six figures or have every detail figured out to get started. If you're just beginning your financial journey, even small, consistent savings at your current age can make a big difference over time. If you're further along but haven't taken full control of the wealth building aspect of your financial house, now's the time. Every small step you take today is an investment in the life you want for tomorrow.

Follow these basic disciplines with your financial professional:

Increase Your Financial Education

The more you know about money, investing, and financial strategies, the more empowered you'll be.

Save and Invest Consistently

Even if it's just a little a month, it can add up fast when you factor in compounding interest.

Set Clear, Realistic Financial Goals

Setting specific targets helps you confidently navigate toward your desired financial destination.

Review Goals and Progress at Least Once a Year

Review performance to spot any trends that may require action to stay on track with your goals.

Make Adjustments as Your Life and Finances Change

If needed, adapt your strategy to stay on track toward your goals.

You've got the power, the time, and the ability to create a future you'll be proud of. So, let's get to it—you and your older, wiser self are so worth it. Contact your financial professional today.

Wealth Building Threats We Must Confront and Conquer

There are three threats to building wealth that many of us young adults don't often consider—we just weren't taught about them. And that's totally fine! The important thing is that we're gaining awareness now so we can tackle these obstacles head-on.

Here's the overview—then we'll dig in to each one:

The Impact of Taxes

Sales tax isn't sneaky—you see it right there on your receipt. But income tax? That can quietly eat away at your cash flow and come back to haunt you years down the road. Imagine being in your late 60's, only to realize you owe 20-30% in taxes on your $1 million nest egg. Suddenly, that's $200,000 or $300,000 gone. Whether you face a tax advantage or a tax disaster in the future depends on understanding your paycheck, withholdings, and the financial choices and tax strategies you implement today.

The Impact of Inflation

Over the last century, the cost of things has risen by about 2.8% per year, thanks to inflation. So, let's say you think you'll need $1 million for retirement in 25 years. If inflation keeps up at that same rate, your estimate is way off. In reality, you'd need almost $2 million, not $1 million, just to keep up with the rising cost of living.

The Impact of Losses

Between 2000 and 2010, the stock market dropped 50% in value—twice. Yep, you read that right. For families relying on steady investment returns to meet their goals, those years were brutal. Warren Buffett famously said, "Rule number one, never lose money. Rule number two, never forget rule number one." It's a reminder that strategies to protect your wealth are crucial, and shouldn't be overlooked.

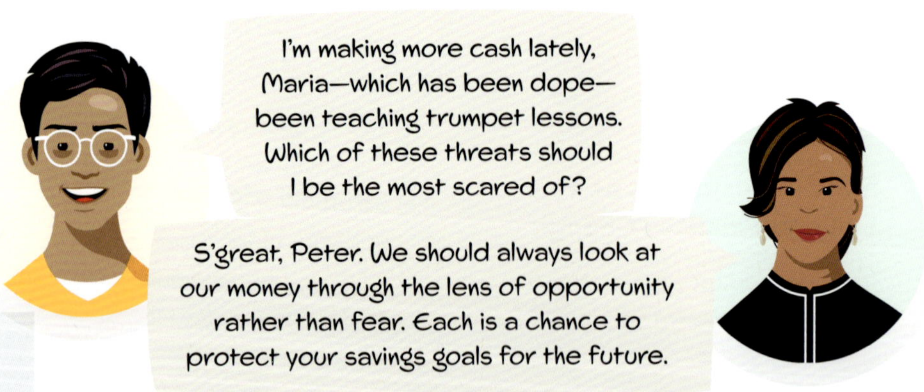

THE IMPACT OF

Taxes

Taxes seem like one of the most painful topics to cover, but we promise, this chapter will really make you feel like you have the 411 when you're done reading it.

There are two different tax roads we'll go down here:

1. Some quick highlights regarding the taxes you pay to federal and state governments on your salary, wages, and income annually
2. How earnings from various investment accounts are taxed

Let's start with the first road...

Your April 15th adult obligations

Tax Day is usually April 15th, but look up the exact date each year—the IRS sometimes changes the due date due to federal holidays or rare factors like Covid-19 for tax years 2019 and 2020. You can request an extension if you need more time, but an important detail to keep in mind—you'll still need to pay any taxes owed by the original deadline.

What important documents do you need to gather?

- W-2 form(s) from any job(s) you had
- 1099 form(s) if you're a freelancer, independent contractor, or earned interest/dividends
- Student loan interest statements (Form 1098-E), if applicable
- Tuition statements (Form 1098-T) if you're still in school or recently attended
- Proof of any other income (like investments or rental income)

A Quick Note About Your Paystub

Ever wondered how much you've paid in taxes or what your employer takes out of your paycheck? Your pay stub has the answers. It's a breakdown of your earnings, showing your gross income (before deductions) and all taxes and withholdings. Taking a few minutes to review it helps you understand where your money is going and is the starting point for taking more control over your finances.

Take a look at the example paystub below and get to know the various taxes and deductions that are removed from your pay.

ChitChat Accounting *51-2322286*
2240 Carlonius Street,
Whitmer, NY 20234

Earnings Statement
Stub Number: **245**

Employee Info	SSN	Pay Schedule	Pay Period	Pay Date
Amy Fabersmith (Emp.ID:STS001) 102 Main Street, Kalibast, NY 20211	XXX-XX-7889	Weekly	Feb 19, 2025 to Feb 25, 2025	Feb 26, 2025

Earnings	Rate	Hours	Total	YTD	Taxes / Deductions	Current	YTD
Regular Earnings	$10.00	40 hrs	$400.00	$3,200	Federal Withholdings	$44.50	$356.00
					FICA - Social Security	$24.80	$198.40
					FICA - Medicare	$5.80	$46.40
					State Witholding	$20.00	$160.00
					Employer Taxes		
					FUTA	$24.80	$198.40
					SUTA	$44.50	$356.00

YTD Gross	YTD Taxes / Deductions	YTD Net Pay	Gross	Taxes / Deductions	Net Pay
$3,200.00	$760.80	$2,439.20	$400.00	$95.10	**$304.90**

- **Federal & State Withholdings:** The amount of federal and state income tax withheld from your paycheck and is based on the amount you earn and the info you gave your employer on your W-4.
- **FICA–Social Security:** FICA (Federal Insurance Contributions Act) is a U.S. federal payroll tax deducted from each paycheck. This is how you earn credits for Social Security benefits.
- **FICA–Medicare:** This is the other portion of your FICA tax which is used to cover Federal Medicare programs which you will be eligible for around 65 years of age.
- **FUTA & SUTA:** These are mandatory taxes your employer must pay to fund Federal (FUTA) and State (SUTA) unemployment programs.

What Are Deductions?

- Deductions are basically magic for your taxes—they let you subtract certain expenses from your income, which lowers your 'taxable' income—the portion Uncle Sam can tax.
- Most young adults go with the standard deduction because it's straightforward and works for most people starting out.
- Education credits are a big deal if you're paying for college. Look into the American Opportunity Tax Credit or the Lifetime Learning Credit to save some cash.
- Got student loans? You might be able to deduct the interest you've paid (up to a certain limit). It's a small win, but every bit helps!
- If you're a 1099 contractor or freelancer, you've hit the deduction jackpot! From home office costs to business expenses, there are many options. Online resources and a CPA can help you figure it all out. Just remember—the more deductions you find, the less tax you owe! Here is a good starting place to learn more: irs.gov/credits-deductions/businesses

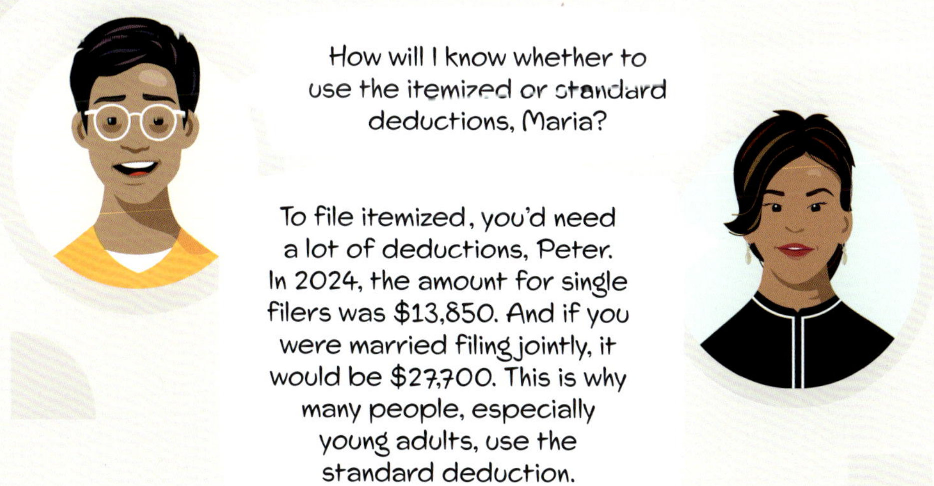

Thanks for explaining that, Maria. It's important to note that the threshold for standardized deductions changes annually. Just do a quick search to find out what it is for the current tax year.

How do you file? Here are your options...

- You can use online software like Intuit, TurboTax, H&R Block, etc. Most offer free filing for simple returns or for a low price that can actually be used as a write off next year.
- Hire a Tax Professional: If your taxes are more complicated, consider hiring a CPA—like Maria.
- If your income is below a certain threshold, you may qualify for free filing through IRS Free File. Look up online, "what is the income threshold for IRS free filing for the current tax year."

Once you finish filing, how do you get your refund or pay what you owe?

- Track your refund status using the IRS "Where's My Refund?" tool. You have the option to get a direct deposit right into your bank account which is usually the most convenient/popular option.
- If you owe taxes, you can pay right away through your tax software as one of your final steps. If you work with a tax professional, they will walk you through how to pay by the deadline to avoid penalties.

How do you stay organized for next year?

- Keep one physical folder for all your tax mail that you receive (like your W-2) and keep one digital folder in your Dropbox/Google Drive... any one location basically for all your tax-related documents and receipts (screenshots work great) so they're easy to find next tax season.
- If you want some extra credit, we highly recommend looking up a sample free spreadsheet to keep track of all of your expenses, especially if you are self-employed. We can't tell you how much easier a spreadsheet makes it to plug all your numbers into your tax software... makes the whole process significantly smoother. There are also some cool apps that can track expenses.

Now that you have the basics on how to be a responsible tax-paying adult, let's talk about the second tax road: **how savings and investment accounts are taxed.**

You pay taxes to federal and state governments on your salary, wages, and income on an annual basis. This section is not about that. It focuses on how earnings from various savings and investment vehicles are taxed. When you know how these taxes work, you're better equipped to make decisions with your financial professional about which strategies are the most advantageous for you.

The 3 Different Ways Savings and Investment Accounts Are Taxed

Tax Now *(Taxable)*
With accounts of this type, you pay taxes on interest, earnings, and dividends every single year.

Examples
- Stocks and Bonds
- Mutual Funds
- Savings Accounts
- Certificates of Deposit (CDs)

Tax Later *(Tax-Deferred)*
With accounts of this type, you're not taxed until you start taking distributions in retirement.

Examples
- Traditional IRAs
- 401(k)s and 403(b)s
- Annuities

Tax Never *(Tax-Free)*
With accounts of this type, your earnings and distributions are never taxed.

Examples
- Roth IRAs
- Permanent Life Insurance
- Municipal Bonds
- College Savings Plans

The Seed vs. The Harvest

One of the big questions to answer is when you want to pay taxes. Consider this example: If you save $10,000 at age 29 and earn a 9% annual return each year, you would have $250,000 when you reach 65. Would you rather pay taxes on...

The Seed
Using post-tax contributions for the initial $10,000 allows for all of the money—most importantly the compounded growth—to be accessed tax-free in retirement.

The Harvest
Paying tax on the $250,000 harvest means all your earnings will be taxed—and you'll pay the future tax rate, which could be higher.

How Taxes Affect Various Savings and Investment Accounts[26]

Taxable Accounts

With taxable accounts, you make an investment with money that has already been taxed—income you've earned from your business, or salary and wages from employment. You pay taxes annually on the interest and dividends your accounts earn unless held in qualified retirement plans.

Qualified Retirement Plans

With 401(k), 403(b), 457, and IRA plans, your pre-tax dollars grow without having to pay taxes on the principal or growth until retirement, at which time you'll pay income tax at the future tax rate on the full amount of distributions each year.

Annuities

Money invested in an annuity—except for qualified retirement plans—will have already been taxed. The growth in an annuity is tax-deferred until retirement. At that time, you'll pay income taxes on the growth portion of your distributions each year.

Government Bonds

You use after-tax money to invest in government and municipal bonds (excluding qualified retirement plans). The interest on federal government bonds is taxable at the federal level, but not at the state and local level. Conversely, the interest on municipal bonds is exempt from federal income tax. If you live in the state in which the municipal bond is issued, you can also avoid state and local taxes.

Roth IRAs

You invest in a Roth IRA with after-tax dollars. Your account grows tax-free and you don't pay taxes on distributions in retirement. Unfortunately, the IRS limits the use of Roth IRAs to people below a specific income level and restricts the annual amount they can add to their accounts.

Permanent Life Insurance

Premiums are paid with after-tax dollars. As long as your policy remains active, you will never pay taxes on distributions you take for supplemental retirement income or special purchases. Distributions, however, will reduce your death benefit. The IRS doesn't limit the annual amount you can contribute or restrict income levels for eligibility, which is why permanent life insurance is often referred to as the 'Roth IRA for the wealthy.'

2 People, Same Savings, Same Return—One Costly Mistake

Before moving on from the tax conversation, it's important to see just how costly it can be when taxes aren't factored into financial decisions. Here's an example of an expensive tax mistake that makes it crystal clear...

Both Val and Maria invest $6,000 per year, from age 25 to 65 (40 years), and earn an average 9% annual return compounded annually. Assume that Val's taxable account is subject to a blended Federal and State tax rate of 20% resulting in a net annual return of around 7.2% compounded annually.

Details	Val TAXABLE ACCOUNT	Maria ROTH IRA ACCOUNT
Total Contribution	$240,000	$240,000
Accumulation Period	40 years	40 years
Annual Return	9% before tax (approx. 7.2% after taxes)	9%
Total Value at Age 65	**$1,358,135**	**$2,215,752**
4% Annual Distribution for 25 years	$54,325	$88,630

At age 65, Val and Maria decide to begin taking annual distributions at the rate of 4% of their total value. Assuming no further growth in their accounts, their retirement funds will last for the next 25 years. However, Maria will retire with more than 1.5 times the spendable cash Val will have. Val had to pay taxes yearly on gains, while Maria paid taxes upfront and was able to let her money grow. Ask your financial professional how you might qualify to use vehicles like Roth IRAs, employer-sponsored qualified plans, and permanent life insurance.

This example is for illustrative purposes only and does not guarantee future results. The calculations are based on an assumed tax rate and assumed rates of return and do not reflect actual market performance. Investment returns are subject to market fluctuations, and principal values may increase or decrease. Actual results may vary due to fees, taxes, and other factors. Past performance is not indicative of future results. Please consult a financial professional before making investment decisions.

THE IMPACT OF

Inflation

We hear about inflation all the time on the news and in politics. But should we actually pay attention to it?

Spoiler alert: yes, we should—but let's break it down so we're all on the same page. Inflation is the rate at which the prices of goods and services rise, which reduces the purchasing power of your money over time. In simple terms, inflation makes your money worth less—what you can buy today with $100 will cost more in the future.

Key Term Alert: Consumer Price Index (CPI)

The CPI is a way to measure inflation. It tracks the average change in prices over time for a 'basket' of goods and services that urban consumers typically buy. Think of it as a key indicator of how expensive life is getting.

How Inflation Works

When inflation happens, each dollar you have buys less over time. For example, if inflation is 3% per year, something that costs $100 today will cost $103 next year. Over time, that adds up. Have you noticed how much gas or groceries cost now compared to a few years ago? It's wild to think that $20 in 1990 had the same buying power as about $46 today.

What's the Solution? Outpace Inflation.

Notice the word 'outpace'—this isn't about just surviving inflation; it's about staying ahead of it. *Here's how:*

- **Increase your income.** Having multiple streams of income is a great way to offset rising costs and give yourself financial breathing room.
- **Make smart money decisions.** Look for ways to save and invest wisely to grow your money faster than inflation eats away at it.

Inflation might seem intimidating, but the key is to understand it and take steps to ensure your financial growth outpaces its effects. With a solid plan, you can handle rising prices like a pro.

> **Inflation is the parent of unemployment and the unseen robber of those who have saved.**
>
> — MARGARET THATCHER

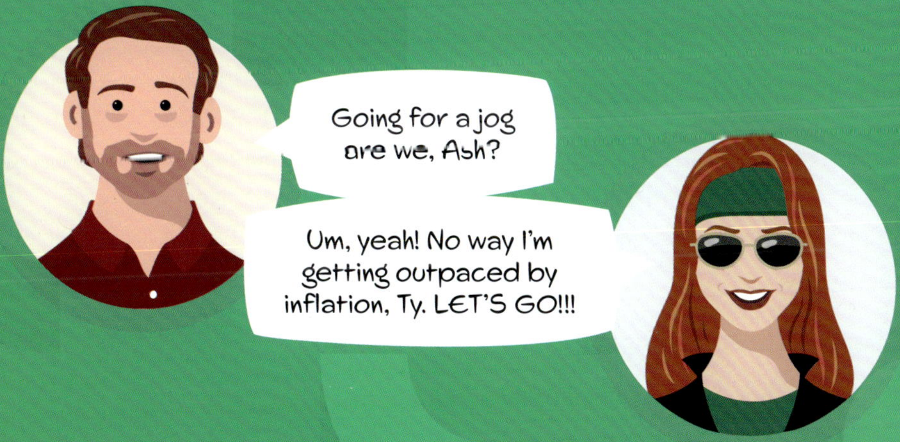

Great attitiude, Ashley! Rather than being alarmed by Margaret Thatcher's words, we should be prepared by factoring the impact of inflation into our savings and investment strategy.

THE IMPACT OF

Losses

Quick quiz—suppose you lost 50% of a $10,000 investment...

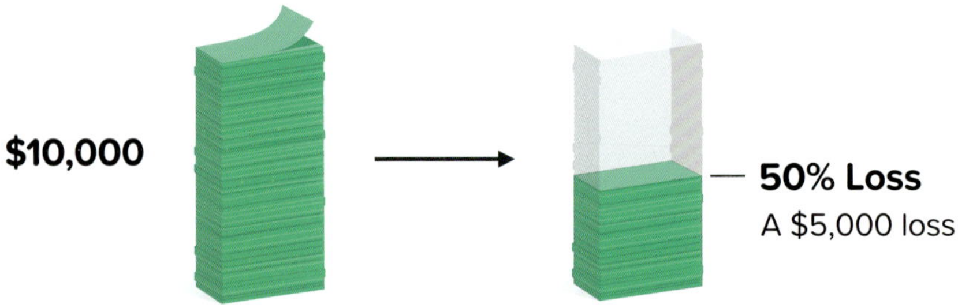

To get back to $10,000, would you need a gain of 50% or 100%?

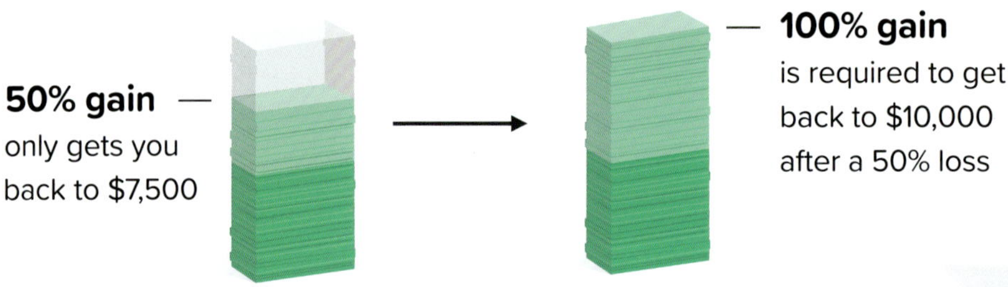

During the ten years between 2000 and 2010 the stock market lost 50% of its value twice. Years of money growth disappeared overnight. Nest eggs and dreams for retirement vanished. Major setbacks like these—and even minor losses—can throw off your savings goals and ruin your plans for the future.

Strategies to Protect Against The Impact of Losses

- Stick to low-risk investments if you want to avoid big losses—but just know they don't grow your money as fast.
- Mix it up! Spread your investments across different industries and risk levels. That's called diversification, and it's like not putting all your eggs in one basket.
- Look into options that let you enjoy market gains while minimizing market losses. Yep, they're a thing!
- ACT NOW: Consider taxes, think about inflation, and check in with your financial professional for solid guidance about reducing the impact of losses.

Will You Run Out of Money in Retirement?

We're not too young to think about creating a guaranteed income for our retirement years—in fact, now is the perfect time. Why? Because... TIME!

Many employees today rely on a combination of 401(k) plans and Social Security benefits to provide enough money to live on in retirement. The average 401(k) balance for baby boomers ages 61-88 is $250,900.[27] The average income of 65-year-olds is $54,860.[28] That's almost exactly a fourth of their 401(k) balance. So how many years will their 401(k) last?

Let's say you only live on 50% of the $54,860 income you had before retiring—that's $27,430 per year. If you factored in 3% inflation and you could get a 6% annual return on your 401(k) account which is worth $250,900, you would run out of money in approximately 10 years.[29] That means if you started taking out distributions at age 67, your 401(k) would be gone by age 77. What if you lived until you were 85 or 95? Will Social Security alone be enough? Who knows?

When your retirement income isn't guaranteed, we leave ourselves open to a really scary scenario—being in our late 70's or 80's without any income!

In a recent Gallup survey,[30] 85% of non-retired American investors strongly agreed that having a guaranteed income stream in retirement to supplement Social Security benefits is critical.

You know what it takes to build wealth, and you're totally aware of the things that can mess it up. But let's be real—making your money last as long as you do? That feels like an even bigger challenge. Especially since retirement these days can last 20, 30, or even 40 years. So, where do you even start?

First, sit down with your financial professional and figure out your chances of running out of money based on where you're at right now. Once you've got that picture, you can look into ways to set up a steady, reliable monthly retirement income to help lessen the risk of running out of money. The good news? If you start early, you've still got time to make it happen!

Milestone 7

FORTIFY

Wealth Protection

Okay, let's talk about estate plans. Sounds like something old people with mansions worry about, right? Nope! It's actually something very relevant to young adults. Fear not—it's not nearly as intimidating or complicated as it sounds. It's just about the best way to protect your assets, your loved ones, and your future. And by assets, we're referring to any cash you have stashed in your checking, savings, and investment accounts—AND—all of your personal belongings that have value to you or your family (like your jewelry, that trading card collection in your closet, the home gym you built during COVID, and Nana's antique dining room table you inherited), and any real estate you own.

But it's not just about who gets your stuff. Your estate plan also includes decisions about your healthcare and finances in case you're ever unable to make them yourself. It's really about making things easier for the people you care about and avoiding unnecessary stress for your family or legal drama later on.

We know. It feels like you have plenty of time to figure this out later. But it's infinitely better to have it taken care of now than to leave your family guessing. Estate planning isn't just about protecting your money; it's about making sure your wishes are followed and the people you love are cared for.

Like we said, it's straightforward when explained, we promise—it's just one of those smart money moves that's crucial to get done NOW.

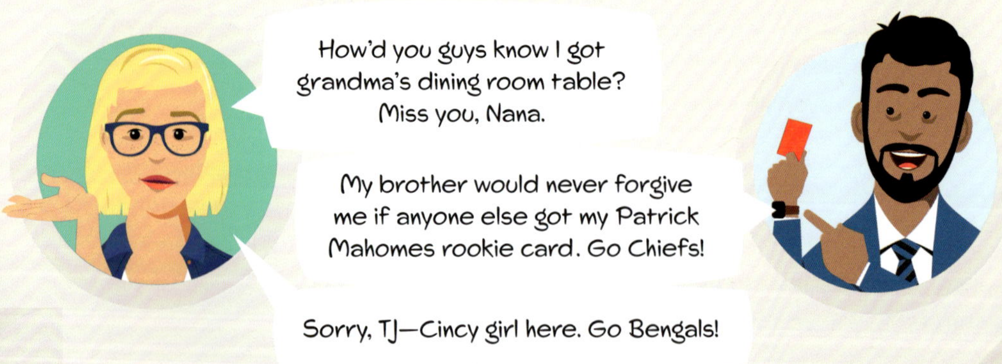

4 Documents Your Estate Plan Should Include[26]

Will

Identifies who will be the guardian of your minor or special needs children, who you want to carry out your wishes, and how you want your property distributed

Financial Power of Attorney

Gives your spouse or other trusted person control over your financial affairs, like paying your bills, insurance, taxes, or selling your property, if you're unable to do it yourself

Advance Healthcare Directive or Living Will

Identifies the person you want to make your healthcare decisions if you cannot and states what medical treatment you wish to receive if you're unable to choose

Health Insurance Portability and Accountability Act

Permits your healthcare agent to legally access your medical records and insurance information to facilitate your medical treatment

Without an estate plan, things can go seriously wrong. First off, your wishes might not be followed, and instead, a court could end up deciding who gets your stuff and who takes care of your kids. That's called probate—and it can be a nightmare. It can take forever, cost a lot, and stress out the people you love. Plus, without an estate plan, your family could end up fighting over what to do with your stuff, your health, and your kids.

Unless you're a teenager, all of us should ACT NOW on this one so your wishes are clear, and your family won't have to deal with unnecessary heartache or drama. It's just the right thing to do for yourself and everyone you love.

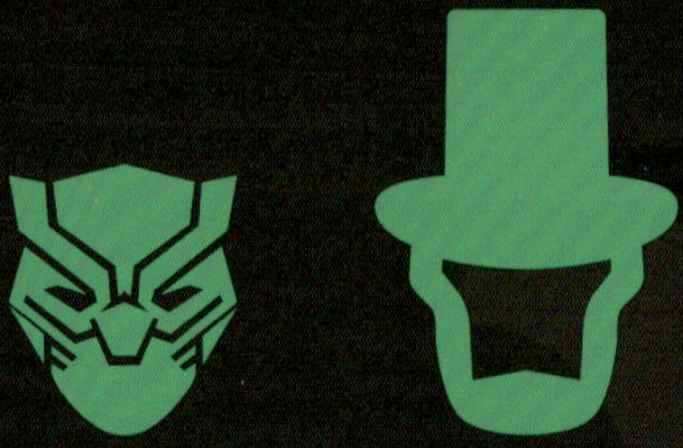

Many well-known, wealthy individuals have passed away without an estate plan or will, leading to heartbreak, family drama, and costly legal battles.

Chadwick Boseman, the beloved actor who played Black Panther, didn't have a will to outline his wishes for his $2.3 million estate. Neither did Abraham Lincoln, despite being an attorney himself.

These examples show how important it is to have your affairs in order, no matter how famous or wealthy you are. We don't just do it because it's an essential Money Milestone. We put our estate plan in place because of how much we love our family and friends and care about their future.

> **"The best way to protect the future is to create it.**
>
> – ABRAHAM LINCOLN

It's a famous quote, but maybe he should've created his estate plan.

Even if you have a will, some of your assets may still have to go through probate before your loved ones can get their hands on them. And if you own property in different states, your estate might have to go through probate in each of those places—talk about a headache! But don't worry, there's a simple way to save your family and business partners from all that hassle and extra cost: one more estate planning tool that can make a huge difference.

It's called a trust. It can...

- Manage your property after you become physically or cognitively impaired
- Protect the interests of your children who are currently incapable of handling money due to age, immaturity, disability, illness, or substance abuse
- Protect special needs children and beneficiaries from losing eligibility for government benefits
- Provide privacy since the trust is not filed with the probate court
- Avoid probate in multiple states if you own real estate in more than one state
- Lower your estate taxes and provide added tax advantages for large estates

Here's the thing: some assets, like life insurance, IRAs, 401(k)s, and certain bank accounts, go straight to your named beneficiaries when you die. They don't need to go through a will or trust. And if you co-own anything with someone, like a house or car, it'll automatically go to them when you pass.

Now, we know you might be thinking getting an estate plan set up is going to cost a lot of money or take forever. However, it's nothing compared to the time and money your loved ones could waste if you don't ACT NOW. Whether you go with a local attorney or an online service, there are options for every budget. Don't let your family and friends PAY LATER—get this Milestone completed and check it off the list!

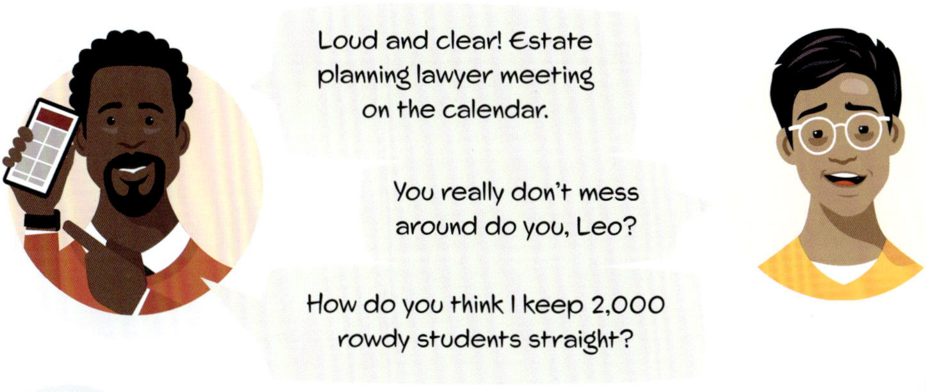

ACT NOW

- ✓ Find a financial professional you like and can trust.
- ✓ Gain a thorough education of the 7 Money Milestones with urgency—time is of the essence.
- ✓ Develop a plan of action with your financial professional to complete each Milestone, knowing you don't have to do them in order—you just have to do them well.

PAY LATER

- ✗ Put the Milestones off because you're too busy right now.
- ✗ Complete the first 5 short-term Milestones but disregard the final 2 as tasks to complete when you're older.
- ✗ Go it alone. Trusting someone else with your money isn't going to work for you.

FIRSTS

Your First Car and House

IT'S TIME TO BUY

Your First Car

Yes, buying your first car is a big deal! And sure, it probably means taking on a car loan (we got into that in Money Milestone 4)—and yeah, it can feel a little intimidating to commit to something this major. But with the right guidance, it doesn't have to be stressful—it can actually be enjoyable! Let's look at some key questions you should ask yourself, resources to help you along the way, and tips to make the process easier. With these tools, you'll be hitting the road in your new ride in no time.

Begin by writing down your answers to these ***3 Key Car Buying Questions:***

1. **What is your budget?** Start by setting a realistic budget that includes not only the car's price but also the cost of insurance, fuel, maintenance, and unexpected repairs.

2. **Should you buy a new or used car?** New cars come with warranties and the latest features, while used cars can cost less upfront and lose their value more slowly. Explore both options.

3. **How long do you plan to keep the car?** A longer ownership period may justify a higher upfront cost for reliability and features. For a short-term purchase, resale value and lower upfront cost should be your top concerns.

Once you've answered these key questions, it's time to dive into the buying process. Get ready to leverage the best tools and strategies savvy buyers use to stay informed and snag a great deal.

Utilize and cross-reference the info from these dependable resources:

- **edmunds.com:** Use this website to compare car prices, read expert reviews, and check out detailed specifications to help you make an informed decision and find the best deal for your first car.
- **consumerreports.org:** We think this web service is worth its relatively small subscription cost. The site gives you access to their in-depth reliability ratings, safety scores, and performance reviews for different car models. Their expert analysis can help you make a well-informed choice and avoid models that tested poorly.
- **carfax.com:** On their site, you can check a vehicle's history report, which provides important information about past accidents, title status, and previous ownership. This helps ensure you're making a safe, informed decision, especially when buying a used car. Auto dealerships typically offer free Carfax reports for the inventory on their website. If you're buying from an independent seller, you may have to pay carfax.com for the history report. Knowing the history of a car is almost always worth it.

Once you've selected your car, it's time to navigate financing for your car. This is not a time to take anyone's word for anything. It's a time to be astute and advocate for your needs.

Arm yourself with these insights as you approach financing:

- **First-time Car Buyer Incentives:** Many lenders offer special programs for first-time buyers with limited credit, including benefits like lower down payments, interest rates, and more flexible qualification criteria, sometimes even offering rates as low as 0% for those with good credit.
- **Larger Downpayments:** One way to lower your monthly payment and save on the cost of car loan interest is to put down as much money as you can when buying the car. If this is a good option for you, consider delaying the purchase until you have the downpayment that meets your goals.
- **Financing Length:** The more years you opt to pay off your loan, the smaller your monthly payments will be. This can be very tempting! Just know that the fewer years you finance your car, the less you'll pay in interest.

YOU'RE READY TO PURCHASE

Your First House

Buying your first house is a huge achievement, and we've already covered a lot about mortgages in Money Milestone 4, but if you need a refresher, definitely check it out again. Let's quickly go over three critical factors to keep in mind as a first-time homebuyer:

1. **Set a total home-ownership financial plan.** Included should be your downpayment, total cost of your mortgage including interest, and your estimated monthly mortgage payment. Don't forget closing costs, homeowners insurance, property taxes, and other homeownership expenses like HOA fees, repairs, and maintenance. The key here is to understand the total cost of owning a home instead of making the short-sighted mistake of only considering a monthly mortgage cost that fits your budget.

2. **Factor in PMI.** If you're putting down less than 20%, you'll also need to factor in PMI (Private Mortgage Insurance), which will be added to your monthly mortgage payment until you have 20% equity in your home. Keep an eye on this, so you can remove it as soon as you hit that 20% mark. You'll need to be proactive by requesting your lender to remove it.

3 **Get Pre-Approved Before You Start House Hunting.** Getting pre-approved by a lender is super important because it strengthens your offer and helps you understand your budget. When shopping around for a mortgage, compare rates from multiple lenders to find the best deal, and make sure to check your credit score beforehand—this will influence your interest rate.

Before you sign to buy the house, consider inspecting the property a little further to make sure you get the best deal before and after you take over ownership. Search the internet for a checklist of items to look into, questions to ask, and clever moves to make to maximize your home ownership value.

Here's a quick checklist to get started:

- Request a professional inspection to uncover potential issues with the roof, foundation, or electrical systems that could affect value.
- Make sure the home's plumbing and HVAC systems are in working order, as repairs can be expensive and affect your home's livability.
- Review the home's energy efficiency, as improvements like upgraded insulation or windows can save you money long-term.
- Have the septic system inspected (if the property is not on sewer). If the system is full, you can request that the seller pay the cost of emptying the septic tank.
- Consider the neighborhood's growth potential—if it's in a developing area, it could increase the home's future value.
- Research the local schools and amenities—homes in areas with good schools and nearby conveniences tend to hold or increase in value.
- Meet the neighbors. Strike up a conversation with someone who lives on the street of the home you're considering.
- Consider driving distances. Is this close enough to your workplace, school, church, and family?

ACT NOW

- ✓ Before falling in love with a car or home, set a budget.
- ✓ Seek consultation from a friend or family member who knows a lot about buying cars or homes. Buy them lunch and pick their brain.
- ✓ Do everything you can to remove emotion from the financial side of the car and home buying process.

PAY LATER

- ✗ Look only at the monthly payment to determine if you can afford a car loan or mortgage instead of the full cost that will impact your finances.
- ✗ Trust any seller or real estate agent to have your best interests in mind instead of sticking to your goals, knowing your needs, and advocating for yourself.

FIRSTS

Getting Married and Merging Finances

YOU SAID "I DO" TO

Getting Married and Merging Finances

The event of marriage can be one of the most exciting times of your life! It's also a time when a lot of changes happen really quickly—including shifts in your financial situation. Marriage usually means you're going from managing just your income to becoming a 'household' with two incomes!

So, how do you make decisions together?

There's no 'one size fits all' approach here. We wish there was! Money is super personal for both individuals and couples, so the best advice is to stay open-minded and be willing to experiment with different strategies for managing finances as a team. Being flexible and communicative will help reduce stress and allow you both to figure out what works best for your relationship.

Once you're back from the honeymoon, sit down together as newlyweds and commit to being intentional about making your financial life a top priority. Or even better, get into the habit of having financial discussions right after you get engaged.

Should you combine bank accounts? It's a big question, and every couple handles it differently. Factors like career specifics, debts, and spending habits can all influence the decision.

The key is to have an open discussion about the pros and cons based on your unique situation. The most important thing is being on the same page and communicating openly. Many couples get stuck because they're afraid to talk about it, but once the conversation happens, it's often much easier than expected. Just remember, being a team is what matters most.

Marriage money topics to work out—and even try out:

- **Sit down together regularly.** Have weekly or monthly 'financial check-ins' to talk about bills, budgets, and upcoming needs or wants.
- **Appoint a 'Chief Financial Officer.'** The CFO of the household is the one who will take charge of managing the budget and paying bills. This person should always consult their partner, but ultimately holds the responsibility for setting meetings and taking action.
- **Test out different budgeting methods as a couple.** Maybe one of you loves spreadsheets and the other is all about using an app with a sleek design. Compromise and agree on the tool that helps you both stay on track. Also, don't forget to set up an emergency fund to cover 3-6 months of income—just in case life throws you a curveball.
- **Establish the discipline of quarterly check-ins.** Have a quarterly meeting to examine your financial goals—short-term (1-3 years), mid-term (5-8 years), and long-term (10+ years)—both individually and as a couple. Write your goals down to increase your chances of achieving them! Plus, it's fun to see how your goals evolve over time.

Decide which of these accounts you will join together or keep separate:

- *Checking Accounts*
- *Savings Accounts*
- *Investment Accounts*
- *Credit Cards*

These accounts are typically separate by nature:

- *Life Insurance*
- *Retirement Accounts (e.g., IRAs, 401(k)s, 403(b)s)*

Now that you're married, be sure to update your beneficiary designations.

ACT NOW

- ✓ Seek financial counseling before marriage.
- ✓ Be intentional about your short-term and long-term financial goals early—even before the wedding—and continue to meet for regular reviews into marriage.
- ✓ Establish who will be the primary person to manage the week to week finances and budget.

PAY LATER

- ✗ Ignore the discomfort and awkwardness of discussing money before the wedding and after.
- ✗ Fail to set budgets and financial savings goals.
- ✗ Keep all your accounts separate or join them all together without thoughtful discussion.

FIRSTS

Making a Career Change

THE DAY HAS COME FOR

Making a Career Change

So you've decided it's time to switch careers, industries, or even make the move into entrepreneurship for the first time. Good for you! It's exciting, but pay careful attention to how this change will impact things like your benefits, health insurance, and retirement savings.

Here's a quick tip on your retirement accounts: If you have a 401(k) or other retirement plan with your previous job, you'll need to figure out what to do with those funds. You may be able to keep the money in the existing plan, or you can roll the funds over into your new employer's plan or an Individual Retirement Account (IRA) that you own directly, instead of leaving them with your old employer. Discuss your options with a financial professional to determine what would be best for you. Keep track of all your retirement accounts.

When choosing a retirement plan at your new job, take time to explore the available options—develop an understanding of the investment choices, fees, and features. It's a great idea to consult a financial professional—maybe even the one who gave you this book—to help you evaluate your options and create a strategy to maximize your retirement savings.

If you're venturing into entrepreneurship, remember you won't have access to traditional retirement options like a 401(k) anymore. You're now fully responsible for building and managing your retirement savings. The key is setting up personal retirement accounts, like an IRA, SIMPLE 401(k), SEP IRA, and continuing the habit of paying yourself first.

More considerations for new entrepreneurs to work through:

- **Cash Flow Management:** Understand your business's revenue cycles and ensure you have sufficient cash flow to cover both business and personal expenses, especially during slower periods.
- **Health Insurance:** Transitioning to self-employment means losing employer-sponsored health insurance. Explore options through the Health Insurance Marketplace, private insurers, or a spouse's plan to ensure uninterrupted coverage. There are consultants to help with this too.
- **Business and Personal Expenses:** Separate your personal and business finances by opening a dedicated business account and tracking expenses carefully. This distinction is essential for tax purposes and financial clarity.
- **Income Tax Strategy:** As an entrepreneur, you're responsible for estimating and paying quarterly taxes. Work with a tax professional to understand deductions, credits, and strategies to minimize your tax burden while staying compliant.
- **Credit Score Maintenance:** Your personal credit score can affect your ability to secure business loans or lines of credit. Monitor and maintain a good credit score by paying bills on time and keeping credit utilization low.

When I got my first big pay bump as a principal, I went a little wild. I saw the bigger paycheck and thought, 'Why not?' Now I've learned that anytime you start making more money, the first thing you should do is revisit your budget—control your money before it controls you.

My issue was similar but kind of the reverse, Leo. When I switched from a job to my own business, I made less for a while. I overspent too! It took me a minute to see that I needed to adjust my budget for less income.

ACT NOW

- ✅ Be proactive about rolling over your 401(k) from your previous employer into an IRA, making sure you know the terms and specifics regarding the new rollover account.
- ✅ Get help and take the time when selecting compensation and retirement plan options with your new employer.
- ✅ Find a mentor to help you navigate entrepreneurship.

PAY LATER

- ❎ Lose track of your rollover from your previous employer.
- ❎ Ignore the importance of adjusting your budget when making more or less money at your new job or when starting your new business.
- ❎ Assume you can wear all the hats at your new business and manage the stress without help.

FIRSTS

You've Started a Family

READY OR NOT—YOU'VE

Started a Family

Talking to your kids about money can feel so intimidating—especially if you're still figuring out your own finances. Every parent wants to set their kids up for success and give them better opportunities than they had, but how do you teach essential money skills when you didn't get that guidance growing up? When's the right time to start these conversations?

Let's be real: money can be a pretty heavy topic. If you grew up in a household where it caused constant stress, arguments, or tension, that experience can really shape your relationship with money as an adult. Many people struggle to shift their money mindset because of how tight things were growing up or because of the negative dynamics they witnessed.

On the flip side, we've also met plenty of people who had the opposite experience—where money was never a struggle—but they still didn't get taught about it. Instead, their understanding of money came from watching the adults in their life and how they handled it. And here's the thing: whether money was stressful or just a background thing, it often wasn't talked about openly and honestly.

Recognizing this is actually super empowering. Why? Because it means you have the chance to create a different narrative for your kids. Modeling a healthy, balanced relationship with money can be more impactful than any lesson you sit down and teach them. Make money a normal, positive topic in your household—not something surrounded by stress or secrecy. Encourage curiosity. Let your kids ask questions, and answer them in an honest, age-appropriate way.

You have the chance to help your children see money differently right from the start. Instead of growing up with a scarcity mindset—where money feels like this mysterious thing that only rich people have—you can teach them to have an abundance mindset. That way, you'll help them believe they can always earn enough, save enough, and have enough. You'll help them avoid stress about running out, and they'll even expect that one day they'll be able to share that abundance with others.

Here are some ideas that can be helpful ways to create a positive environment for your children surrounding money:

- **Start simple.** Share basic concepts like saving, spending, and sharing. Make it casual and fun by bringing it into playtime—like when you're playing kitchen or ice cream shop. Show them how saving works using clear jars or a savings app so they can watch their money grow. Help them set short-term goals, like saving for a toy, and long-term ones, like a trip to the zoo, to teach patience and planning.
- **Keep it engaging.** Utilize games, books, and apps that make money fun. Monopoly (in kid-friendly versions) and apps like Greenlight are great tools. An allowance is also a practical way to teach saving and budgeting. They'll make mistakes, but that's part of the learning process. The key is being consistent—pick a method and stick to it so they know what to expect.
- **Try a clever allowance idea.** One easy option is giving them their age in dollars weekly—$5 for a 5-year-old, for example. As they get older, give them more responsibility, like managing their own money for clothes or outings, so they learn to prioritize needs versus wants. Start with cash so they understand its value, then transition to virtual options to mirror how money works in the real world.
- **Introduce bonus rewards.** For a real-world feel, try a bonus system instead of an allowance. Pay them for completing chores or extra tasks, with higher rewards for more challenging work. It's a great way to teach the value of effort while making it fun and productive—plus, you might get a little extra help around the house!

- **Involve older kids.** As your kids get older, include them in budget decisions, like planning a grocery trip or family outing within a set amount. Let them make decisions and see how far their money can go. For summer camp, they can shop for supplies on a budget to practice resourcefulness and creativity. You may be surprised how much they enjoy it!

- **Don't underestimate your teens.** When they're teens, start conversations about bigger topics like investing, credit, and debt. Books like *How Money Works: Stop Being a Sucker* can make these concepts easier to understand.

- **Teach generosity.** Teach your kids the joy of sharing one's wealth—not just the mechanics of saving and spending. Encourage them to set aside money for giving—it could be donating to a cause or helping someone in need. Showing them the joy of giving keeps money in perspective and builds compassion. When you model generosity for your kids early on, you're instilling values they'll carry with them for a lifetime.

Not true, Peter. Even if you'll have to spend all your savings in your retirement years, you can still pass a legacy to your kids financially. You just have to do one thing every time you have a child—ACT NOW!

MILLION DOLLAR BABY®

The Gift of a Future

Million Dollar Baby is a common sense strategy that empowers families to create a legacy for their children without having to be wealthy. It's time to rethink how parents leave a legacy.

> **"Only 26% of study participants said they expect to leave behind an inheritance. This will disappoint many millennials and members of Generation Z.[31]**
>
> — NORTHWESTERN MUTUAL'S '2024 PLANNING & PROGRESS STUDY'

The traditional inheritance model went something like this: Parents would save diligently throughout their lives. In retirement, they'd rely on their pension and social security, carefully preserving their savings to leave as an inheritance for their children. After their passing, often in their mid-70's, their children would split the inheritance—using it to save for their future, buy a house, pay for their kids' education, or make other big purchases, depending on the amount.

Today, however, people are living much longer—well into their late 70's, 80's, and even 90's. These extended lifespans come with higher medical expenses and greater long-term care needs, meaning retirees often need to rely on their savings to cover these costs. As a result, leaving a substantial inheritance for the next generation has become unrealistic for most families.

Enter the Million Dollar Baby Strategy

So, if people are unable to leave an inheritance to their adult children because they need to live on their retirement savings to afford a longer life, how can they contribute financially to their children at the end of their lives?

They can't.

That's where the Million Dollar Baby strategy totally changes the game. It literally flips the old inheritance model on its head. Here's how it works: When the baby is born, parents, grandparents, or other family members contribute a small amount into an investment account.

Then, over the course of the baby's entire life—60 or 70 years—that money grows thanks to the magic of compound interest. By the time they hit retirement age, they've become... a Million Dollar Baby. That small contribution from their family decades earlier has turned into a massive retirement fund worth a million dollars (or more!).

Why didn't anyone think of that before?

As always, you can **ACT NOW or PAY LATER.**

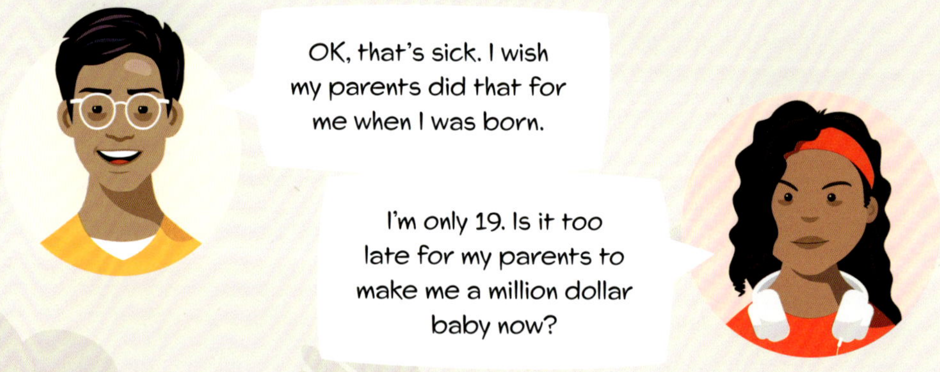

Time makes all the difference, Zoey.
Check it out...

The Difference 18 Years Can Make

Take a look at the hypothetical examples[7] below. In the first scenario, the parents of a baby girl put down a one-time lump sum of $13,000 on the day of the baby's birth. The money grows at a 7% average annual interest rate, compounded annually. By the time the baby turns 67, the money has grown to over $1,000,000.

Now what if the parents waited until the baby turned 18 to put down the one-time lump sum of $13,000 with the same rate of return? The baby would only have $334,476 when she turned 67. That's almost an $800,000 difference. The Million Dollar Baby example works best if you wait until the child reaches retirement age before taking withdrawls.

If parents are unable to make a one-time contribution when their baby is born, they can still achieve a similar result by making monthly contributions to the Million Dollar Baby strategy for a few years. For example, if the parents and grandparents can contribute a lump sum of $2,500 at the baby's birth and then add $250 per month for the next 4 years, their child would have $1,101,081 by the time the child turns 67. This scenario assumes an average annual interest rate of 7%, compounded annually. A scenario like this may be more realistic for some families.

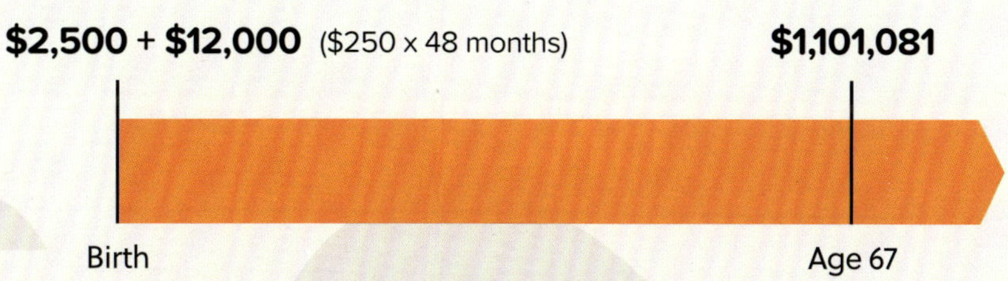

There's a variety of ways the Million Dollar Baby strategy can be structured for families.

If you want to give your children the gift of a future, reach out to your financial professional today to create a plan that works for YOU!

MILLION DOLLAR BABY®

ACT NOW

- ✓ Assist your child with using a portion of their allowance to save towards a specific goal.
- ✓ Include your children in family money decisions, habits, budgeting, and discussions.
- ✓ Gather the family to discuss how to leverage the Million Dollar Baby strategy when your child is born.

PAY LATER

- ✗ Expect your child's school to cover everything in their one semester personal finance class.
- ✗ Consider your child too young to appreciate or understand basic money concepts.
- ✗ Hope you can save enough over the course of your life to create both a retirement income for yourself and an inheritance for your children.

Next Steps

Congratulations! You've taken the first step toward building a financial future that works for you. By learning how money works, you've already gained something most people never do—the tools and knowledge to make informed financial decisions. Now, it's time to put that knowledge into action.

The earlier you start, the more powerful your decisions become. Time is your greatest asset, and every dollar saved or invested today has the potential to multiply tomorrow. But taking control of your money isn't just about numbers; it's about creating a life of freedom, opportunity, and confidence.

Where to begin? To start building your financial foundation, here's a step-by-step plan...

Keep a step-by-step plan to start building your financial foundation:

- **Know where you stand:** Take inventory of your current finances—your income, expenses, debts, and savings. Understanding your starting point is the first step.
- **Set smart financial goals:** Identify what you want to achieve in the short-term (e.g., build an emergency fund), medium-term (e.g., save for a down payment), and long-term (e.g., retirement).
- **Create a budget that works for you:** Make every dollar intentional. Track your spending. Prioritize saving and investing. It's OK to start small.
- **Build an emergency fund:** Life happens. Save at least three months' worth of income to cover unexpected situations.
- **Invest early and consistently**: Small amounts invested consistently can grow significantly over time with compound interest.
- **Eliminate bad financial habits:** Avoid high-interest debt, reduce unnecessary expenses, and focus on living within your means.

Collaborate and Share

Taking control of your financial future doesn't have to be a solo journey.

1. **Partner with a Financial Professional**

   Even in the early stages of your financial journey, a trusted financial professional can help you create a personalized roadmap. They'll guide you in areas like debt repayment, investment strategies, and long-term planning, helping to ensure that your choices align with your goals.

2 **Share What You've Learned**

Knowledge is most powerful when it's shared. Start conversations about money with friends, family, or colleagues. By helping others understand financial basics, you'll create a ripple effect that can change lives.

Put Your Knowledge to the Test

Ready to see how much you've learned—and what gaps you still need to fill? Take the Financial Literacy Quiz (taketheflq.com). It's quick, insightful, and designed to help you identify the next steps on your journey to mastering money.

Your Journey Starts Now

Building wealth takes patience and persistence. It's not about being perfect—it's about making progress daily. You have the tools to shape your financial future, and the decisions you make today will create opportunities for years to come.

Know Your Numbers

Understanding your financial goals starts with knowing your numbers. The WealthWave Investment Goal Calculator (investmentgoalcalculator.com) helps you estimate how much you'll need for retirement and the monthly contributions to get there. This easy-to-use tool lets you plan your path to financial independence and align your savings with your long-term goals.

The earlier you act, the stronger your foundation will be, and the more freedom you'll have to live the life you want.

So, ACT NOW! We believe in you—you've got this!

— *Lauren Mathews Fairey & Christa Mathews*

About the Authors

Lauren Mathews Fairey

Lauren Mathews Fairey, in her early 30's, is a dedicated advocate for financial literacy and a voice for the next generation. A Georgia College & State University graduate with degrees in Management and Marketing, Lauren developed her leadership skills through student government, her sorority, being a tour guide, and as a Student Ambassador.

Her career began at one of the world's largest leadership conferences, followed by marketing roles where she helped grow small businesses and became Chief Marketing Officer. This ultimately led her to her passion for financial education. As a Certified Financial Educator®, Lauren teaches young adults and professionals how money works.

Running her WealthWave business and contributing to HQ marketing, Lauren co-hosts WealthWaveLIVE with her sister, Christa, and the WealthWaveNOW podcast, sharing strategies nationwide. Featured in The Wall Street Journal, she's known for making financial concepts relevant and empowering.

Lauren lives in Canton, GA, with her husband Taylor and their three children. Her mission: to inspire the next generation to ACT NOW and take control of their finances to build the future they deserve.

Lauren can be reached at:
lauren@wealthwave.com
wealthwave.com/lauren
howmoneyworks.com/lauren

Christa Mathews

Christa Mathews is a leader in financial education for young adults and families, known for her relatable approach to a vital life skill. In her late 20's, she has already built a reputation as a trusted advocate for empowering the next generation with financial literacy.

A graduate of Georgia College & State University, Christa honed her leadership and creativity skills as a Tour Guide, Student Ambassador, and event photographer. After graduating, she joined WealthWave's HQ team, developing innovative digital marketing and content strategies to connect with younger audiences. Licensed as a Certified Financial Educator®, Christa simplifies financial concepts for emerging generations and mentors professionals on using digital tools to promote financial literacy.

As a co-host of WealthWaveLIVE, a guest on major TV networks, and host of WealthWaveNOW podcasts, Christa inspires audiences nationwide. Also an experienced photographer, Christa infuses her teachings with the same vision and clarity she brings to her lens, inspiring others to envision and shape their financial futures with confidence.

Christa's mission is to equip young adults with the tools they need to overcome financial challenges, take control of their money, and create the lives they deserve.

Christa can be reached at:
christa@wealthwave.com
wealthwave.com/christa
howmoneyworks.com/christa
christaclear.com

Behind the Creative

Andy can be reached at:
andy@wealthwave.com

Andy Horner

Andy is the Chief Marketing and Technology Officer at WealthWave. He and his team have helped financial educators build their brand, tell their story, teach their students, and serve their clients with world-class design, marketing systems, and digital tools for over 12 years. He is a co-author and the creative lead of the book, *HowMoneyWorks: Stop Being a Sucker*, which has now sold almost a million copies. He is also a co-author and the creative lead of the book, *Change Your Literacy, Change Your Life: Begin Your Personal Financial Revolution.*

Andy is a graduate of Virginia Commonwealth University, where he studied Communication Arts and Design. Before starting his own company, he led creative at a variety of ad agencies and web design studios. Today, WealthWave offers a wide range of software and agent marketing services, from websites, campaign and social media management, brand development and online sales tools, all the way to video production.

A storyteller at heart, Andy is developing a series of fiction novels for teens in his spare time. He lives in Atlanta, GA with his wife, Tonia, and their four sons.

Resources and Disclosures

1. National Financial Educators Council, "Financial Illiteracy: Research, Data, Definition, & Opinion," (2022). https://www.financialeducatorscouncil.org/financial-illiteracy/
2. National Financial Educators Council, "Financial Literacy and the Revival of the American Dream," Vince Shorb (Aug 2016). https://www.financialeducatorscouncil.org/wp-content/uploads/2016/08/financial_literacy-1.pdf
3. World Economic Forum, "Can you answer these 3 questions about your finances? The majority of US adults cannot," Michelle Meineke (Apr 24, 2024). https://www.weforum.org/stories/2024/04/financial-literacy-money-education/
4. Springer Nature Link, "Is Financial Capability a Determinant of Health? Theory and Evidence," Sicong Sun and Yu-Chih Chen (Nov 2022). https://link.springer.com/article/10.1007/s10834-022-09869-6
5. National Endowment for Financial Education, "Respect Legislative Intent with youth Financial Education Requirements," Billy J. Hensley (Aug 19, 2024). https://www.nefe.org/news/2024/08/respect-legislative-intent-with-youth-financial-education-requirements.aspx
6. Education Week, "A Few Years Ago, 8 States Required Personal Finance Education, Now It's Up to Half," Elizabeth Heubeck (Jan 11, 2024). https://www.edweek.org/teaching-learning/a-few-years-ago-8-states-required-personal-finance-education-now-its-up-to-half/2024/01
7. This is a hypothetical scenario for illustration purposes only and does not represent an actual investment in any product. Actual investments can fluctuate in value and there is no assurance that these results can or will be achieved. It does not include performance risks, expenses, fees or taxes associated with any actual investment, which would lower results. Rate of return is an assumed constant nominal rate, compounded monthly. It is unlikely that any one rate of return will be sustained over time. Investing entails risk, including possible loss of principal. Numbers are rounded to the nearest dollar in some cases. Retirement needs vary by income and cost of living—$1 million isn't an adequate goal for every saver.
8. CNBC MakeIt, "Every young person should see this chart to understand their 'greatest money-making asset,'" Ryan Ermey (Aug 12, 2022). https://www.cnbc.com/2022/08/12/chart-why-an-investors-greatest-asset-is-time.html
9. These examples are for illustrative purposes only and do not guarantee future results. The calculations are based on assumed rates of return and do not reflect actual market performance. Investment returns are subject to market fluctuations, and principal values may increase or decrease. Actual results may vary due to fees, taxes, and other factors. Past performance is not indicative of future results. Please consult a financial professional before making investment decisions.
10. ValuePenguin/LendingTree, "Consumer Banking: Statistics and Trends," Richard Zhang (Nov 26, 2024). https://www.valuepenguin.com/banking/average-bank-interest-rates#:~:text=Average%20interest%20rates%20at%20major%20U.S.%20banks%20,%20%200.25%25%20%206%20more%20rows%20
11. Federal Reserve, "Money Stock Measures – H.6 Release," (Dec 26, 2024). https://www.federalreserve.gov/releases/h6/current/
12. WalletHub, "Average Credit Card Interest Rates," Adam McCann (Jan 13, 2025). https://wallethub.com/edu/cc/average-credit-card-interest-rate/50841
13. Bankrate, "47% of Americans overestimate life insurance costs – here's why it's actually affordable," Ashlyn Brooks (Oct 14, 2024). https://www.aol.com/finance/47-americans-overestimate-life-insurance-173925559.html
14. The Zebra, "How much does a funeral cost? A complete breakdown," Susan Meyer (Apr 19, 2024). https://www.thezebra.com/resources/personal-finance/how-much-does-a-funeral-cost/
15. Forbes, "Living Paycheck to Paycheck Statistics 2024," Emily Batdorf (Apr 2, 2024). https://www.forbes.com/advisor/banking/living-paycheck-to-paycheck-statistics-2024/
16. Forbes, "Student Loan Crisis Grows As Families Could Take On Record Debt in 2024," Robert Farrington (Mar 21, 2024). https://www.forbes.com/sites/robertfarrington/2024/03/21/student-loan-crisis-grows-as-families-take-on-record-debt-in-2024/

17. Diverse Education, "Chaos and Confusion: The State of Student Loans," Liann Herder (Jul 5, 2024). https://www.diverseeducation.com/students/article/15679040/chaos-and-confusion-the-state-of-student-loans
18. Pew Research Center, "5 facts about student loans," Richard Fry and Anthony Cilluffo (Sept 18, 2024). https://www.pewresearch.org/short-reads/2024/09/18/facts-about-student-loans/
19. Education Data Initiative, "Average Student Loan Interest Rate," Melanie Hanson (Jan 8, 2025). https://educationdata.org/average-student-loan-interest-rate
20. Consumer Financial Protection Bureau, "Choosing a loan that's right for you." https://www.consumerfinance.gov/paying-for-college/choose-a-student-loan/
21. Experian, "Average Credit Card Debt by Age in 2024," Chris Horymski (Jul 2, 2024). https://www.experian.com/blogs/ask-experian/research/credit-card-debt-by-age/
22. Experian, "What are the different credit score ranges," Louis DeNicola (Dec 18, 2024). https://www.experian.com/blogs/ask-experian/infographic-what-are-the-different-scoring-ranges/
23. LendingTree, "Car Depreciation: How Much Is My Car Worth?," Lauren Nicholson (Apr 29, 2024). https://www.lendingtree.com/auto/how-much-do-new-cars-depreciate/
24. National Library of Medicine, "Impact of financial literacy, mental budgeting and self-control on financial wellbeing: Mediating impact of investment decision making," Ruofan Bai (Nov 14, 2023). https://pubmed.ncbi.nlm.nih.gov/37963159/
25. YNAB, "7 Budgeting Challenges in the First Three Months," Ben Barlowe (Jan 18, 2022). https://www.ynab.com/blog/7-budgeting-challenges
26. "How Money Works for the Next Generation: Act Now or Pay Later" does not provide tax or legal advice. Please consult with your personal tax and/or legal professional for guidance on your particular situation.
27. Fidelity, "How do your retirement savings stack up?," 2024. https://www.fidelity.com/learning-center/personal-finance/average-retirement-savings
28. USA Today, "Average salary in the U.S. in 2025," Mehdi Punjwani and Sierra Campbell (Sept 26, 2024). https://www.usatoday.com/money/blueprint/business/hr-payroll/average-salary-us/
29. Sharebuilder, "How Long Will My 401(k) Savings Last?," Permanent Online Calculator. https://www.sharebuilder401k.com/help/401k-income/
30. Gallup, "Investors Want Freedom With Retirement Savings," Lydia Saad (Jan 5, 2018). https://news.gallup.com/poll/225023/investors-no-strings-attached-retirement-income-stream.aspx
31. ThinkAdvisor, "Only a Quarter of Americans Expect to Leave an Inheritance," Michael S. Fischer (Aug 6, 2024). https://www.thinkadvisor.com/2024/08/06/only-a-quarter-of-americans-expect-to-leave-an-inheritance/

Lauren Mathews Fairey is a registered representative of Transamerica Financial Advisors, Inc. (TFA). WealthWave Media, LLC (WM) is not affiliated in any way with TFA. This book was written by Lauren Mathews Fairey under an arrangement with WM and not as a representative of TFA. This book was published by and is owned by WM.

TheMoneyBooks Series—Complete Your Collection

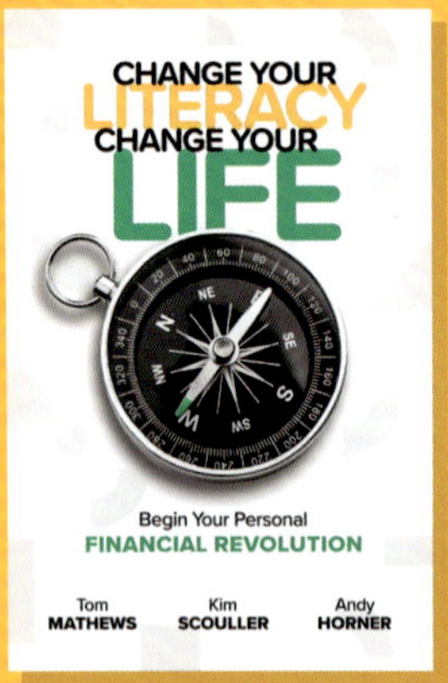

Your Financial Literacy Journey Begins Here

Discover all the ways knowing how money works can shape your well-being and help secure the future you've always imagined.

The Foundation For Your Financial Education

Make sure you read the original book that's changing how financial education is taught everywhere.

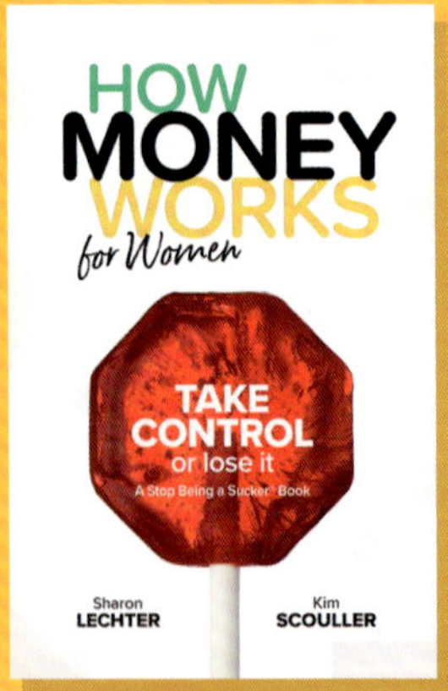

Financial Empowerment Belongs to Us

Don't miss our book designed to empower women to achieve financial success at every stage of life.

Ask for a copy from a financial educator who teaches from TheMoneyBooks Series today.

Discover your financial literacy level.
You're a Financial Pioneer.
You're a Financial Trailblazer.
You're a Financial Learner.
You're a Financial Starter.
You're a Financial Beginner.
FINANCIAL LITERACY INDEX
Financial Literacy Quiz
3 Reasons to Take The Quiz
Financial Literacy Quiz
TAKE THE QUIZ NOW—TAKETHEFLQ.COM

What Financial Leaders Are Saying

"Starting early with financial knowledge is one of the most impactful decisions anyone can make. This book gives young people the tools to turn time into their greatest asset.

— **TOM MATHEWS,** CO-AUTHOR OF *HOW MONEY WORKS: STOP BEING A SUCKER*

"I've seen firsthand the transformative power of financial literacy for young people. This book takes a complex topic and makes it simple, offering readers a clear path to financial confidence.

— **MARISSA MITCHELL,** FINANCIAL EDUCATOR

"The 7 Money Milestones alone make this book worth reading. They provide a practical, step-by-step guide that any young person can start using right away.

— **JOSH LITTAUER**, FINANCIAL LEADER

"This book is a game-changer for young adults. The Rule of 72 alone will completely shift how they think about saving and investing.

— **SETH CASALINO**, FINANCIAL EDUCATOR

"Accessible and engaging, this book makes financial education feel like having a personal mentor. It's the perfect guide for young people entering the real world.

— **JAKE REED,** FINANCIAL LEADER

"This isn't just another book—it's a movement to create financially free young people. It will change how you see money forever.

— **CAMERON BERRY,** FINANCIAL EDUCATOR

"As someone who was blessed with parents who taught me about money young, I now teach how important it is to form a positive mindset about money early in life. This book is the ultimate guide for young adults to create an abundance mindset, to avoid pitfalls, and build a lasting legacy.

— **SHARON LECHTER,** CO-AUTHOR OF *HOWMONEYWORKS FOR WOMEN* AND *RICH DAD, POOR DAD*

"The strategies in this book aren't just theory—they're life-changing steps that will transform how the next generation approaches money.

— **KIM SCOULLER,** CO-AUTHOR OF *HOWMONEYWORKS FOR WOMEN*

"As a young entrepreneur, this book gave me the tools to balance investing in my business while preparing for the future. It's truly life-changing.

— **GIANMARCO CACCIAMATTA,** FINANCIAL LEADER

"The lessons on budgeting and cash flow are practical and easy to implement. For the first time, people will feel in control of their finances.

— **MELANIE DYSON**, FINANCIAL EDUCATOR

"Managing student loans can be overwhelming, but this book shows people how to tackle debt while building wealth. It can give you hope and direction.

— **KENDAL MCCRAY,** FINANCIAL EDUCATOR

"The chapter on compound interest blew my mind. It completely changes how people will think about money and time—it's never too early to start.

— **CHAD OLSEN,** FINANCIAL LEADER

> Financial literacy isn't just about numbers—it's about confidence. This book teaches young people how to make choices that will shape their future.
>
> —**BILL MITCHELL,** FINANCIAL INDUSTRY LEADER

> This book makes financial literacy exciting, relatable, and actionable. It's a wake-up call for young people to take charge of their financial future.
>
> — **MARCUS MITCHELL,** FINANCIAL EDUCATOR

> Finally, a book that makes financial literacy approachable and empowering for young people. It's the roadmap we've all been waiting for.
>
> — **SAM KNICKERBOCKER**, FINANCIAL EDUCATOR

> This book is a must-read for young professionals. It equips you with the clarity and tools to make your money work for you—not the other way around.
>
> — **CHANDNI PATEL,** FINANCIAL EDUCATOR

> In today's digital world, managing money is more important than ever. This book combines timeless financial principles with modern strategies, making it essential for young people.
>
> — **MATTHEW SCOULLER,** FINANCIAL EDUCATOR

> As someone who dove into this business full-time, I can confidently say this book provides the foundation every young person needs to build real wealth.
>
> — **DANNY LANSKEY,** FINANCIAL LEADER

> If only I had read this book before earning my first paycheck—it could have saved me countless hours. An essential read for anyone in their 20's.
>
> — **JOSH SCHWIETERMAN**, FINANCIAL LEADER

> This book doesn't just teach about money—it teaches mindset. It's a guide for navigating early adulthood with intention and purpose.
>
> — **HOLLY BOCHSLER,** FINANCIAL EDUCATOR

> This book is full of lessons I wish I'd learned in school. It's the financial education I'll be teaching my kids.
>
> — **DELANEY RIPPLE,** FINANCIAL EDUCATOR

> Every young adult deserves to feel empowered about their finances. This book breaks down complex topics into clear, actionable steps for success.
>
> — **TREVOR NERDIN,** FINANCIAL LEADER

My mom and Aunt Christa wrote an amazing book to teach young people about money! Now I know saving dollars can make them grow—it's like planting money seeds!

— Harper Fairey

(Lauren Mathews Fairey's Daughter)